WHALE
QUEST

Working Together to Save Endangered Species

KAREN ROMANO YOUNG

For Joanne

Acknowledgments for help and support: Deborah Kovacs; and for being a wonderful part of this book, Roy Ahmagoak, Chad Avellar, Mark Baumgartner, Séan Bercaw, Domenica Di Piazza, Elysa Engelman, Sarah Wilson Finstuen, Susan Funk, Peter Girguis, Courtney Hann, Donna Hauser, Allison Lees Heater, Benny Hopson, Joanne Jarzobski, Kristin Laidre, Greg Marshall, Michael Moore, Ken Ramirez, Frances Robertson,Tracy Romano, Lei Lani Stelle, and Leigh Torres.

Twenty-First Century Books
A division of Lerner Publishing Group, Inc.
241 First Avenue North
Minneapolis, MN 55401 USA

For reading levels and more information, look up this title at www.lernerbooks.com.

Main body text set in Conduit ITC Std 11/15.
Typeface provided by International Typeface Corp.

Library of Congress Cataloging-in-Publication Data

Names: Young, Karen Romano, author.
Title: Whale Quest / Karen Romano Young.
Description: Minneapolis : Twenty-First Century Books, [2017] | Audience: Age 13–18. | Audience: Grade 9 to 12. | Includes bibliographical references and index.
Identifiers: LCCN 2016012561 (print) | LCCN 2016028311 (ebook) | ISBN 9781467792462 (lb : alk. paper) | ISBN 9781512428476 (eb pdf)
Subjects: LCSH: Whales—Juvenile literature.
Classification: LCC QL737.C4 Y68 2017 (print) | LCC QL737.C4 (ebook) | DDC 599.5—dc23

LC record available at https://lccn.loc.gov/2016012561

Manufactured in the United States of America
1-38274-20003-1/19/2017

CONTENTS

OUT OF THE DEEP

Humpback whales come to the surface of the ocean to blow (exhale) air, mucus, and carbon dioxide through the blowhole (nostril) on the top of the head. Adults surface to breathe about every fifteen minutes, though they can remain submerged for almost an hour if necessary.

Whales are visible markers of the ocean life
we cannot see; without them, the sea
might as well be empty for all we know. Yet
they are entirely mutable, dreamlike because
they exist in another world, because they look
like we feel as we float in our dreams.

—Philip Hoare, *The Whale: In Search of the Giants of the Sea*

Sunset off the coast of Cabo San Lucas in northwestern Mexico. A small rubber boat with an outboard motor carries six humans out into the Pacific Ocean. The Sea of Cortez meets the Pacific here, a mating and calving waypoint (a sea landmark) that attracts a pod of humpback whales and their newborn calves, which have been spotted in the area.

Into the water, a naturalist in the boat drops a hydrophone, a microphone that picks up and amplifies the sounds of the whales. Below the surface, the whales of the pod click and "sing" in the low moos and squeals they use to keep in touch with one another. They are saying the equivalent of "Present and accounted for!" or "Come this way." One new mother pushes her baby to the surface, as if presenting him with pride to the human observers.

Above the surface, the humans on this whale watching boat coo and cry out and exclaim to one another. Hearing the whales makes people feel a connection they don't feel every day: connected to Earth, connected to themselves, peaceful and inspired and part of the natural world.

The humpback whales off Cabo San Lucas have traveled here all the way from Alaska to mate and give birth. Along with gray whales, blue whales, orcas, and other whales, they migrate thousands of miles a year between feeding grounds and mating and birthing grounds. Their puffing spouts, splashing tails, and exuberant breaches (leaps out of the water) are familiar to boaters and people onshore.

They've never seen anything like it: a sudden splash, a giant leap, a walloping belly flop back into the sea. Almost all cetaceans (a group of marine mammals including whales, porpoises, and dolphins) breach—and nobody knows why. Could it be to blast off dead skin, dislodging parasites? The force of the fall is strong enough to do that. Could it be showing off, a display of power or attitude? Is it necessary or just fun? Researchers note that younger whales—even calves—breach more than others, lending support to the idea that breaching is a form of play, for fun or to express joy.

SHARING THE SEAS

Throughout history, humans have hunted whales for food, oil for lubrication, fuel for light, and for the natural materials to make brushes, eyeglasses, corsets, and the frames of houses. By the late nineteenth century, humans had overfished whales to the point of extinction. As a result, humans adopted other sources for food, fuel, and materials for shelter and clothing.

The number of whales in the world's oceans, though improved, is still drastically reduced from what it was before whalers decimated their populations. Whales are two of eight Species in the Spotlight, a National Oceanographic and Atmospheric Administration (NOAA) list of species that are the most at risk of extinction. The two whales are Cook Inlet beluga whales, which live off the coast of Anchorage, Alaska, and Southern Resident killer whales, in the Pacific Northwest.

If people don't figure out and protect the conditions that whales need to thrive, the ocean could empty of Earth's largest, most sophisticated aquatic mammal and the ocean's keystone (top) animal in the marine cycle of life. A new challenge faces all earthlings: preserving the health of the ocean. Scientists and conservationists are racing to better understand the way whales live, to anticipate how changes in climate, sea temperature, water chemistry, and pollution could affect whales—and us—forever.

This book is about the many people who watch whales. They include scientists, environmentalists, policy makers, citizen scientists, and friends of whales. Together, they are assessing what whales need—clean, quiet water; a dependable supply of food; the community of other whales; safety; and human respect for their freedom to swim, feed, mate, calve, raise their young, and migrate. Together the whale watchers are telling the stories of whales in the twenty-first century and of the seas we share with them.

CHAPTER ONE
WHAT'S A WHALE?

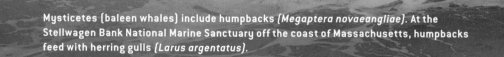

Mysticetes (baleen whales) include humpbacks *(Megaptera novaeangliae)*. At the Stellwagen Bank National Marine Sanctuary off the coast of Massachusetts, humpbacks feed with herring gulls *(Larus argentatus)*.

When you get close to a blue whale and it blows next to you, because it's feeding down there, the blow smells like fish. Whenever I go into a fish market or I smell fish I'm brought back to that moment when I'm on the bow of the ship and a blue whale has just blown next to me. It's such a sight to behold and such a rare privilege.

—Natalie Schmitt, whale geneticist, speaking to Ann Jones, *Off Track*, Australian Broadcasting Corporation, 2015

All life on Earth originally came from the sea. All marine mammals (including polar bears, walruses, seals, and whales) evolved from those early creatures to live on land. Yet they eventually moved back into the sea. Why? Nobody is sure, but some scientific theories indicate that the mammals were following food sources or escaping predators. Over millions of years, the mammals' limbs modified into flippers, and the creatures developed thick skins lined with insulating blubber. They also evolved organs and body systems that gave them the breathing and circulation patterns they needed to make deep dives for food.

A whale travels hundreds—even thousands—of miles between the sites where it eats, mates, and gives birth. These waters range in temperature from arctic to tropical and back again. Equatorial waters are great for wintering, and for mating and delivering new calves, but they are too warm to provide enough to eat. Whales don't starve in these warm waters, though, because they have eaten tremendous amounts of food during the summer season. During summer they live in temperate waters to the north and south that are full of fish. Healthy diets help the whales lay on the blubber that insulates them to keep all systems going as they swim through their seasonal waters.

Of the marine mammals, marine biologists consider whales to be the most highly evolved—the most completely adapted to the marine environment.

Q:

What's the whale's closet relative on land?

A:

The hippopotamus

Scientists estimate that whales transitioned to life in the sea between fifty-five and sixty million years ago. Among the primary environmental changes that impacted whale evolution was a dramatic cooling in sea temperature about thirty-five million years ago. This change killed most reptiles and amphibians yet created an environment rich in the nutrients that krill eat, and these crustaceans are a major food source for whales. As toothed whales evolved, they developed echolocation, the ability to find food and assess surroundings using the echoes of sounds they make. They also developed a larger, more complex brain. Both adaptations helped whales strategize about food and communicate more effectively with one another.

All whales are cetaceans, an order of mammals that lives in the sea. The word *cetacean* is from the Greek word *ketos*, which means "sea monster." Whales are the largest mammals on Earth, and they move through the sea with the propulsion of strong tail flukes, steering with their flippers, and speeded by long streamlined bodies. Unlike fish, they don't have gills to take oxygen from the water. Instead, they have lungs and breathe oxygen from the air through blowholes on the back of their heads. They make dives that vary in duration and depth, according to species.

THE WHALE FAMILY TREE

With more than eighty species, the order Cetacea includes two suborders: Odontoceti (odontocetes), or toothed whales (seventy or more species), and Mysticeti (mysticetes), or baleen whales (thirteen or more species).

Odontocetes have one blowhole. (*Odontos* is the Greek word for "tooth.") They use echolocation to find prey, and they have teeth to catch and eat their food. Toothed whales include dolphins, porpoises, and beaked whales such as pilot whales, sperm whales, and orcas. Odontocetes eat what they can get their teeth around: squid, fish, or seals. Orcas, sometimes known as killer whales,

Dolphins are odontocetes. They are part of the family of toothed cetaceans.

even eat other whales. Toothed whales live in family groups of related whales that may encompass several generations. They establish and follow a leader and stick together even when doing so endangers them all.

Mysticetes are baleen whales. (The word *mysticetes* comes from the Greek *mystakoketos*, which means "mustached whales," a reference to the shape of their mouths.) Baleen whales, also known as rorquals (which describes the ribbing on their bellies), have two blowholes for breathing and are generally larger than toothed whales. Their gaping mouths contain plates of baleen—strips of hard, bristly tissue made from keratin (the same substance in human fingernails). Baleen hangs like the tines of a comb along the whales' U-shaped upper jaw. When a baleen whale opens its mouth, plankton, sand lance, small fish, krill, and other food from the water filters through the baleen. The whales open their mouths so wide that they disarticulate (widen) their jaws, like a snake eating a rabbit, to take a maximum gulp of water with the most potential for taking in large amounts of edible fish. To expel the water, the pleats along the whale belly flatten as they expand, then contract and fold inward. The seawater then flows out through the baleen, leaving the food inside the whale's mouth. Baleen whales may travel on their own or swim with one or two other whales or in larger groups.

WHALE FAMILY TREE

Biological classification is the system scientists use to classify animals according to a hierarchy of related groups, based on similar features. The group at the top of the hierarchy is the largest, whose members share very basic commonalities. The groups at the bottom of the hierarchy share more features. Only animals of the same species can mate and reproduce with one another.

Kingdom	Animalia (animals)
Phylum	Chordata (vertebrates)
Class	Mammalia (mammals)
Order	Artiodactyla (hooved animals, or even-toed ungulates)
Suborder	Whippomorpha (non-extinct whippomorpha, includes whales and hippopotamuses)
Infraorder	Cetacea (whales)
Suborders	Mysticeti (baleen whales), Odontoceti (toothed whales)
Family	Delphinidae (ocean dolphins, family of odontocetes)
Genus	*Cephalorhynchus*
Species	Chilean dolphin (*Cephalorhynchus eutropia*)

WHALE BREATH

About 1,000 miles (1,609 kilometers) north of the northernmost town in North America—Barrow, Alaska—bowhead whales use their bony heads to crack through a fissure in the Arctic ice. They breathe in oxygen and dive down again.

Whales breathe voluntarily, unlike humans, choosing when to breathe. A whale can only breathe at the surface. The exhalation from its blowhole (which is like a nostril) is a blast of seawater vapor, mucus, and carbon dioxide. A blue whale's exhalation measures 1,320 gallons (5,000 liters) in volume. The puff of exhaled air and water is visible miles away, and its shape and height vary with the size and species of whale. Experienced whale watchers look for a whale's exhalation spout from a distance—"thar she blows!"—and they can also identify the species by the spout.

At the surface of the water, whales exhale until they have blown out all the carbon dioxide in their lungs and then fully reoxygenated to recharge their bodies. To dive back into the water, whales collapse their lungs and suck in their ribs, forcing a large amount of air into the skull. This method allows the animal to dive deeply and, when ready, to come up to the surface quickly without getting the bends, or decompression sickness. Were a human diver to resurface from as deep down as a whale—and as quickly—that person's lungs would explode, and the person would die.

Whales are the world's largest living creature. The brain size of whales and dolphins, in ratio to their total body size, is large—second only to the human brain/body ratio. Scientists have found that the brains of humans and other primates have spindle cells, which are associated with complex social behaviors such as empathy (the ability to understand a situation from someone else's point of view). These cells are also part of the brains of dolphins and many species of whales, both odontocetes and mysticetes, which are not primates.

Q:

Do toothed whales get cavities?

A:

Yes

Toothed whales, such as this orca (*Orcinus orcas*) off the coast of British Columbia in Canada, have one blowhole for breathing. Baleen whales have two.

WHALE TO WATCH: BAYLA, NORTH ATLANTIC RIGHT WHALE

Whales are routinely caught in fishing nets and other potentially fatal debris. If a whale cannot escape, it will die from lack of food, from cuts and other wounds caused by the gear, from infection, or from all of these. Rescue teams all over the world try to release entangled whales every day. The first course of action when a rescue team reaches an entangled whale is to attach a sea buoy and line to her so that the team can track her movements. They do this because they expect the whale to swim away while the team is removing the gear in which the whale is caught, and the gear may need to be removed in steps. The members photograph the whale, assess the extent and location of her entanglement, and form a strategy for removing it. The team may sedate the

A team works to free a whale caught in fishing gear. They use a pole to attach a suction cup that records data about a whale's body orientation and depth in the water. The team then uses a dart gun to give the whale a sedative. Calmed, the whale allows the team to remove almost all the fishing gear.

Whales exhibit complex social interactions and behaviors. And they show an impressive ability to communicate and to learn, change, and adapt songs and other auditory signals. That's why marine biologists believe that whales are extremely intelligent.

BIG CHARMERS

Whales play a major role in the ocean. They are keystone animals—species at the top of the food chain. Their health is an important indicator of the overall health of the ocean food chain and of the marine habitat in which they live. Whales have another role that is vitally important. Like sharks, polar bears, sea turtles, tigers, wolves, and other especially fascinating animals, whales are charismatic megafauna—a term scientists use to whale so the members can do their work without further harming the animal.

Biologist Michael Moore, a biologist at Woods Hole Oceanographic Institution (WHOI) in Woods Hole, Massachusetts, found a medication and developed a method for sedating distressed whales. The sedative is so powerful that it could kill a person even if it only dripped on skin. Moore found the right dosage to quiet a whale for ninety minutes, which is usually long enough for a team to cut a quiet whale free of entangling gear.

SWIMMING WITH A HEAVY LOAD

In 2014 rescue teams off the coast of Florida spied a North Atlantic right whale known as Bayla. She was snared in lines that snaked through her mouth and around her body and in gear that dragged behind her. She had been swimming with this heavy load for months, the lines gouging her flesh and threatening to pull her down.

Moore raced to Florida to help the exhausted whale. From an inflatable boat behind Bayla, he fired his sedative-loaded dart. He watched as Bayla swam on, straight and calm, not bolting or panicking. The rescue team could then slip knives inside the entangling lines and gear to cut them loose. Bayla swam away, free.

Yet Bayla's story was not over. A few days later, a dead whale washed ashore. It was Bayla. Her necropsy (physical exam after death) revealed that her cause of death was lacerations or infections from ropes that her rescuers had not been able to see.

describe gorgeous, big, awe-inspiring animals with many, many human fans.

Since the 1970s, humans have changed their relationship with whales, hunting them less and studying them more. The whale watch industry has ballooned, with thousands of boats worldwide taking humans out onto ocean waters to observe whales in the wild. Marine biologists who observe and study whales have enlisted citizen whale watchers to help them see, hear, and understand the mammals even better. People also watch whales when they visit them in aquariums and zoos. As these whale watchers learn about whales, they learn about ocean life in general, gaining an understanding of the condition of the sea and of the issues humans face in caring for it. And they teach their children, who bring new imaginations, ideas, and intelligences to work on making the world a healthier place for whales and people alike.

WHALE TALES

As charismatic megafauna, whales have captured the human imagination for centuries. They appear in sacred texts, literature, television, movies, and other media. Here's a brief sampling of some intriguing whale tales, from oldest to most recent:

Jonah and the Whale

This is a famous story from the Book of Jonah in the Old Testament of the Hebrew Bible. Jonah is the central character of the tale. As a test of Jonah's faith in God, he is cast overboard into the sea and survives three days in the stomach of a whale. Then the tale says that "the Lord spake unto the fish, and it vomited out Jonah upon the dry land." Despite enduring hardship, Jonah's faith in God is not shaken.

Moby Dick

American writer Herman Melville based his 1851 novel *Moby Dick* on his experiences on a whaling voyage. Literary scholars consider it to be one of the great American novels for the way it deals with the theme of humanity struggling with nature. The novel points to the sacrifices whalers made in hunting whales for their valuable oil.

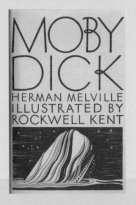

Flipper

This popular television series ran from 1964 until 1967. The stories revolved around two boys, the sons of the warden of a marine preserve, who become friends with a bottlenose dolphin on the island of Coral Key, Florida.

The Voyage of the Mimi

This thirteen-episode educational series ran on public television from 1984 until 1988. It focused on real-life researchers and a group of interested kids who were studying whales together from a sailboat called the *Mimi* in the North Atlantic Ocean.

Whale Rider

In this 2002 film by New Zealand director Niki Caro, Paikea—a young indigenous Whangara girl—rescues a South Pacific right whale.

The Cove

This 2009 documentary by Louie Psihoyos follows a team of activists and scientists who secretly film a cove near Taiji, Japan, where dolphins are herded and then either selected for captivity in water parks or killed for their meat. The Japanese government condemned the film as misleading and insisted that the hunt is carried out legally, although others disagree. This well-reviewed film won an Academy Award for Best Documentary Feature.

Blackfish

This 2013 documentary film by Gabriela Cowperthwaite tells the story of Tilikum, an orca on display at SeaWorld, a San Diego, California, entertainment park. While in captivity there, Tilikum killed three people (two trainers and a trespasser). Experts theorized that the animal had become aggressive as a result of the effects of captivity.

In response to intense public criticism, SeaWorld agreed to discontinue its orca breeding program and promised to build larger aquatic environments for their captive animals. The park faces several lawsuits alleging abuse of animals.

MacGillivray Freeman's *Humpback Whales*

This 2013 documentary film, directed by Greg MacGillivray, reveals surprises about humpback mating, feeding, and entanglement. "When you get that close to a whale . . . your adrenaline is pumping, your heart is pounding and . . . all you do is hope the cameras are working!" says MacGillivray.

CHAPTER TWO

HUNTING DOWN WHALES

In the nineteenth century, New Bedford, Massachusetts, was a whaling hub. Once at sea, whalers would leave their whaleship to hunt from a much smaller whaleboat.

As their land-borne counterparts drove buffalo from sixty million to extinction, so these oceanic cowboys pursued whales to the brink. . . . For America, the common enemy was the wilderness.

—Philip Hoare, *The Whale*

Each March high school biology teacher and whale watch naturalist Joanne Jarzobski of Barnstable, Massachusetts, posts new pictures on Facebook. While walking her dogs on the beach at Race Point, at the tip of Cape Cod, she spots and photographs whales. She first hears, then sees, right whales just beyond the breaking waves. She hears the huff and spray of an exhalation, then the humming inhalation of air through the blowhole. It is, Jarzobski says, her favorite sound in the whole world.

Few whales come this close to shore on purpose, but North Atlantic right whales do. This urban whale, as it is nicknamed, swims not only along remote stretches of coastline such as Race Point. Right whales also swim near shoreline cities, shipping lanes, and harbor entrances. That's one reason they were the "right whale" to hunt at the height of whaling history in the nineteenth century. In fact, because they came so close to populous centers, whalers were easily able to kill them and in such numbers that they were nearly decimated.

This Japanese print from the mid-1800s shows Japanese whalers on the hunt in the East China Sea. Japan continues to whale commercially, despite an international ban.

Inuit women in what later became Alaska cut into a whale caught by whalers in Kotzebue. Whaling is an ancient tradition among indigenous peoples. American photographer Edward Curtis focused much of his life's work on indigenous peoples of North America. He took this photo in about 1929.

Basque whalers who lived along the Bay of Biscay in France once hunted in the eastern Atlantic Ocean. After they had hunted all the whales there, they crossed the Atlantic Ocean in the sixteenth century to whale off the coast of Labrador in eastern Canada. They were the first European whalers to hunt in the western Atlantic. In the twenty-first century, most of the 450 or so right whales in the Atlantic are found in the western part of the ocean.

Europeans are not the only people to have hunted whales. Hundreds of years ago, long before the first European explorers and settlers arrived in North America, indigenous Natick (Wampanoag) people hunted right whales from the shores of Nantucket, an island off Cape Cod that is their homeland. So did many other coastal peoples in coastal Arctic regions and in the Pacific Northwest. Indigenous whalers used harpoons to kill the whales from small boats or from shore and towed the animals' bodies onto the beach to butcher them for food and fuel. They hunted only what they needed to survive, in contrast to later European whalers, who hunted as many animals as they could, for profit.

Pilgrims from England, sailing into Cape Cod Bay on the *Mayflower* in 1620, saw that the Cape Cod right whales were easy pickings. Soon enough, the *Mayflower* was renovated from a transport ship into a whaler.

THE RIGHTER WHALE

Q:

Why were commercial whaleboats made of cedar?

A:

The light, open grain of cedar wood has more cellulose (the material that forms the walls of plant cells) than other woods. It can therefore soak up more water, making it more buoyant.

According to local legend, in 1712 a Nantucket hunter whose sailboat was blown out past the usual distance from shore became the first European to encounter a sperm whale. By then inshore right whale stocks were already low. By the end of the eighteenth century, Nantucket whalers switched to hunting sperm whales and the island had become the world capital of whaling. Sperm whales were even "righter" than right whales. Although they were harder to catch and tow to shore, they had better oil for making candles, and Nantucket candlemakers were the world's best.

In the early nineteenth century, Nantucket's hold on the whaling industry waned. Innovative Basque whalers began to set up enormous cauldrons on the deck of their whaling ships for "trying" in transit. Trying was how whalers boiled blubber into oil. Unlike earlier whalers, the Basque whalers did the trying at sea so that the ships wouldn't have to return to port to process whale blubber there. Other nineteenth-century whalers copied this efficient method. Ships that could hunt, process, and store whale products at sea could stay out for months, following big, oil-rich whales to the farthest reaches of the sea—and hitting the jackpot for the owners of the whaling fleets. The sperm whale was the primary quarry of the whalers. The blubber of other whales could be boiled into oil and even mixed with sperm whale oil (on purpose or as a cheat), but the best oil, spermaceti, came from sperm whales.

Historians consider the 1780s to 1920, when hunting was at its peak, to be the time of the greatest exploitation of whales. Scientists working with the 2003–2013 Census of Marine Life reported about that period, "American whalemen expanded their reach out of the Atlantic and into the Pacific and Indian Oceans, depleting population after population of seven species of whales." The sperm whale, the bowhead, the humpback, the right whale, and the gray whale bore the brunt of the slaughter.

HOW TO HUNT A WHALE

"Whale Ho! Thar she blows!" a spotter would yell from high above the ship's deck in his crow's nest. With the sighting of a whale's spout, little whaleboats would then slide down the davits (small cranes) from the ship into the pitching sea. Each whaleboat's crew of six held on tight: a boat handler (to guide the boat), a boat steerer (to operate the forward oar and harpoon the whale), and four "hands" (to row the boat). The boat steerer's harpoon was ready, and the other men waited for the whale to surface, estimating where and when its dive would end based on the length of its body.

Whaleboats of the nineteenth century were made of light and maneuverable cedar. The bow and the stern of the whaleboat were both pointed.

A whaling team in Arctic waters hoists the jaw (and baleen) of a bowhead whale onto a whaling ship known as the *Beluga*. Once the pieces of the animal were all on board, whalers processed the whale on deck.

WHALE TO WATCH: OMURA'S WHALE

Imagine a whale so rare that people had only seen it as a carcass on the beach, as bones preserved in a museum, or as a skull left behind at a whaling station. That was the case with the Omura's whale until 2013.

That year Salvatore Cerchio, an Italian visiting scientist at the New England Aquarium in Boston, Massachusetts, and his team caught sight of whales with distinctive, uneven coloring near Nosy Be, an island off the northern coast of Madagascar in the Indian Ocean. The team explored the area by boat and encountered forty-four groups of Omura's whales. "When we clearly saw that the right jaw was white, and the left jaw was black, we knew that we were on to something very special," said Cerchio. The team took pictures and underwater videos. They also took biological samples from the whale, using a biopsy dart to gouge out a bit of skin. In the lab, deoxyribonucleic acid (the genetic material DNA) from the samples confirmed what scientists had long suspected. In evolutionary terms, Omura's whales were the first whales of their branch of the whale family. Over time, they adapted to changing conditions to become two new and distinct species: Bryde's and sei whales.

The Omura's whale has close to one hundred distinct throat pleats.

Q:

What happened to the whales that whalers wounded?

A:

Pods of sperm whales would usually stick with a wounded whale. This team behavior actually made it easier for whalers to bring down the whole pod.

This structural feature allowed the boat to go forward or backward to chase a whale. Sperm whales can't see straight ahead or behind them, so good whalemen took advantage of these blind spots to sneak up on the whale. Once the steerer had harpooned a whale, the other men connected it to the boat by the harpoon's long rope line. A harpooned whale could haul the whaleboat by the line, whipping along on what whalers called a Nantucket sleighride, trying to flee at up to 25 miles (40 km) per hour until it was so exhausted the men could draw near and quickly plunge a knife into the animal's heart and lungs.

"Fire in the chimney!" would be the call when the whale's spout filled with blood. The giant animal would experience a "flurry"—a panicked circular swim, accompanied by vomiting and a flippering frenzy. At last, the whale would roll on its side, capsized and dead. The whalers lashed the animal alongside the boat with lines, towing it until they were ready to haul the whale aboard piece by piece. There, the men would skin, slice, and try the blubber in cooking vats on deck. Chunk by chunk, the men butchered the whale's body and boiled the blubber into oil. Whalers tossed overboard whatever they could not use, as food for the birds and sharks.

THE BUSINESS OF WHALING

The Golden Age of Whaling (1820–1860) was the height of whaling as a business, and more than one hundred thousand people worked in the industry. Whaling crews were largely composed of nonwhites from all over the world. Crew members hailed from Africa, the Cape Verde Islands, Polynesia, the Azores, and the United States. Some became captains or mates.

WHALE WATCHER:
NELSON COLE HALEY

Nelson Cole Haley—Nelt for short—was twelve when he ran away from boarding school in Maine to become a whaler. In the mid-nineteenth century, aboard the *Charles W. Morgan*, Nelt was a boat steerer. At the website of Mystic Seaport—a living museum in Connecticut about coastal life in New England—you can read this diary excerpt of Nelt's description of the job:

> The boat-steerer had his first iron [harpoon] in his hand ready to dart, when the whale's head had passed him far enough to reach his body . . . up went his hands grasping firmly the iron, arms extended, body bent back, one foot firmly braced against a cleat [a wooden or metal fixture for holding a line] right thigh set hard into a half circle fitted to each gunwale [the top edge of the side of a boat] . . . the iron was sent with force enough to drive the shank out of sight into the whale's body, like a flash the 2nd iron followed the first, the whale in his pain threw his body half out of the water; with a terrific blow of his fluke he sent a volume of snowy water twenty feet [6 meters] into the air, then disappeared, taking the line so fast out of the boat it burst the loggerhead [a post used to secure the harpoon rope], and caused smoke to rise from the friction. After sounding out about half the line by 100 fathoms [600 feet, or 183 m] he rose to the surface, rolled, tumbled, run his head out of the water, snapped his jaws together, making them sound like pistols' report, now dropping his head underwater with his tail reared aloft ten or fifteen feet [3 to 4.6 m], thrashing the water into foam that would spread over half an acre [0.2 hectares] on the surface. As the other whales went off without our having a chance to strike any of them, we turned our attention to help kill the captured monster.

American whalers included immigrants to the United States, farmers, fishers, American Indians, and blacks who had escaped or been freed from enslavement. Many owners of whaleships were Quakers, who didn't believe in slavery and sometimes turned a blind eye to the possibility that the black people they hired were runaway slaves. (Technically, according to US law then, runaway slaves were to be returned to their legal owners.) One of the most famous whalers was Frederick Douglass, the voice of the abolitionist (antislavery) movement. Douglass had escaped slavery in Maryland in 1838, disguised himself as a sailor, and went to work in the shipyards of New Bedford, Massachusetts, the capital of the whaling industry, where he joined the crew of a whaling ship.

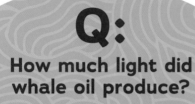

Q:

How much light did whale oil produce?

A:

There are two kinds of whale oil: oil produced from blubber and spermaceti from the head cavity of the sperm whale. Spermaceti candles produced so much more light than those made from whale oil that a new light standard, the lumen, was coined. In the twenty-first century, a single wax candle emits 13 lumens and a 100-watt bulb produces 1,200 lumens.

With more than $100 million invested in workers, thousands of boats, and other whaling supplies, whaling was the fifth-largest industry in the United States. The nation exported 1 million gallons (3.8 million liters) of whale oil to Europe each year. Like many industries, whaling was an owner's game, in which the men who owned whaling ships could expect to earn three times the money they invested in their companies. Cities and towns the length of the eastern seaboard of North America were part of the whale assembly line. In the 1840s, for example, more than half the American whaling fleet sailed from New Bedford to every corner of the globe. Whaling country extended from the waters south of Argentina to those north of Alaska and from the Pacific Ocean west of Hawaii to the Indian Ocean east of Africa.

New Bedford, it was said, lit the world. Whale oil provided the necessary ingredients for lighting, heat, lubrication, and even soap. One bowhead whale could be rendered into one hundred barrels of oil (about 3,150 to 3,500 gallons, or 11,924 to 13,249 liters). Engine parts, clock parts, navigational tools, bicycles, sewing machines, mills, scientific instruments, and telescopes all relied on whale oil, especially sperm oil, to lubricate their parts.

By the end of the nineteenth century, whalers turned from sails to steam to power their ships. Steamboats were faster and more efficient, and they hastened the end for whales and whaling because faster ships meant whalers could chase down and kill more whales in less time. The volume of kill increased exponentially. The steepest decline in whale numbers occurred after 1900. The most popular whales had been decimated, so whalers went after other whale species. Whalers of the new century used high-powered vessels and weapons, taking a large toll from which the whale population is only beginning to recover. In the 1920s, Norway was a leader in new whaling technologies, and Norwegian shipbuilders pioneered the fast and efficient factory ship. However, by then, the world's whale population had been quickly—and significantly—depleted.

By then European American miners had discovered petroleum in the eastern United States. Petroleum-based products such as kerosene, turpentine, alcohol, and lard were making inroads on whale oil. Cheaper than sperm oil, petroleum was used to make plastics, which would replace baleen as a source of eyeglass frames, umbrella spokes, combs, and many other everyday products. Because of the loss of whales and the discovery of cheaper fuel sources, the whaling industry began to die off—just in time to save the animals from complete extinction.

In 1972—after years of public pressure—the US Congress passed the Marine Mammal Protection Act, which finally ended commercial whaling in the United States. The law protects whales, porpoises, dolphins, seals, sea lions, and walruses. In the twenty-first century, about two million whales swim the world's seas. Given that whaling seriously depleted—even wiped out—most whale populations, who can imagine what the oceans were like in pre-whaling days, how full of spouts and song?

CHAPTER THREE
WHALES GET A CLOSER LOOK

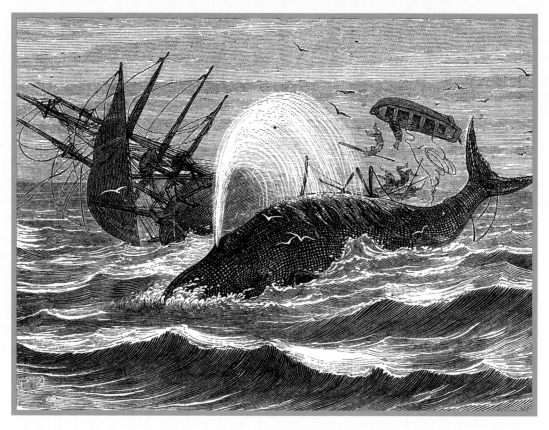

In 1820 a sperm whale rammed and sank the *Essex*, an American whaling ship from Nantucket, Massachusetts. The twenty-man crew was stranded in small whaleboats in the Pacific Ocean for ninety-five days. During that time, the men resorted to cannibalism to survive. The ship's captain—George Pollard Jr.—helped execute and eat his eighteen-year-old cousin. Only eight men survived. The story caught the imagination of the American public and has been the subject of novels, such as *Moby Dick*, fictionalized films, and documentaries.

All of a sudden after World War I [people] woke
up and said there's not many more [whales] out
there. We need to do something to protect them.
The more we saw the way they lived,
the more we cared about them.

—Anne Witty, guest curator, Mystic Seaport, *Voyaging in the
Wake of the Whales* exhibit, 2015

Whales living at the height of the whaling boom in the nineteenth century came to fear and avoid ships, and they sometimes struck back. In 1820 a sperm whale wrecked the whaler *Essex*. Its crew was stranded in the South Pacific and resorted to cannibalism to survive. Some whales grew so aggressive toward whaling ships and so protective of their pods that they became notorious characters, with nicknames such as Tabor Tom, Timor Tom, or Mocha Dick. These melodramatic descriptions and whale tales (tall or true) made monsters of the animals in the public eye. Yet careful observers saw a different, more cooperative creature.

Whalers were the first cetologists, or whale scientists. As they hunted, they observed the close family and social groups in which the whales lived. They saw how the pod shared the upbringing of its calves, protecting one another at their own risk. The whales in each pod hovered in daisy-shaped defense formations—with the calves at the center and the adults ringing them like petals and facing inward, their strong tail flukes to the outside. And they observed the sorrow and abandonment of calves whose mothers had been killed by whalers.

WHERE DID THE WHALES GO?

Whalers knew the sea roads the whales traveled, and they wondered how the animals found their way. In the 1840s, US Navy officer Matthew Maury pored over thousands of old naval ship logs, in which captains had recorded daily

Q:
What do you call a bunch of whales?

A:

POD, OR GAM: up to twenty whales

SCHOOL, OR SHOAL: twenty to fifty whales

HERD, OR BODY: fifty whales or more

events and sightings. Maury used the log entries as raw data to plot the migration paths of whales. He then wrote to whaling captains to ask for details of whale physiology (the function of body parts), the length of their dives, their diets, and much more that he knew could only be gleaned by careful observation. What began as shop talk (sharing of information among people in the same occupation) became the basis of modern whale science. It also yielded some surprises. For example, whalers' logs noted that some bowhead whales that whalers had wounded in the Atlantic Ocean still carried the heads of harpoons when they reached Pacific waters, and vice-versa. Knowing that bowheads, like all whales, have to breathe air, Maury developed a theory that a then undiscovered ice-free passage through the Arctic Circle—commonly referred to as the Northwest Passage—must actually exist. Otherwise, how could the whales get from one ocean to the other? As a result of Maury's knowledge of whales, other explorers renewed their goal of finding the Northwest Passage.

In 1851 whaler Captain Daniel McKenzie sent Maury a letter during a layover in New Bedford. He offered to get blubber samples for Maury from a sperm whale and to provide a description of the whale's physiology. McKenzie was among those who closely observed whales as a business strategy. The captains who knew whale migration routes and had closely observed their behavior were the ones who were most successful at hunting whales.

Not everyone viewed whales as just a source of baleen, also known as whalebone (for corsets, buggy whips, and other things requiring flexible fibers), and blubber (for oil). The European American public of the nineteenth century was fascinated by wild animals. Museum exhibits of large, exotic wild animals toured, drawing large crowds, and zoos were founded to exhibit the animals.

WHALE WE WATCHED: GRANNY (J2)

In May 2014, Captain Simon Pidcock and whale watchers on one of his Ocean EcoVenture tours spotted a 103-year-old orca known as Granny, or J2. She was swimming with her pod of twenty-five, called J-pod, off the coast of Washington State and the Canadian province of British Columbia. J-pod is part of a community of endangered Pacific Ocean whales known as Southern Resident killer (orca) whales. These whales are one of NOAA's Species in the Spotlight, a list of at-risk animals to study and help protect. Southern Resident orcas live in the Salish Sea, in the Pacific Northwest. Northern Resident orcas live along the coast of British Columbia from Vancouver Island to southern Alaska.

Pidcock recognized Granny by her saddle patch, a black-and-white pattern just behind the dorsal fin on the top of her body, and by a nick in that same fin. These two features form an orca's fingerprint—the identifying marks unique to each orca. Ken Balcomb, the executive director of the Center for Whale Research in Friday Harbor, Washington, is among the researchers who study J-pod, which is the most studied pod in the world. He says that in 1976, when researchers first observed Granny, they estimated she was about forty years old.

In the twenty-first century, researchers think that Granny was at least twice the age of Tokitae. That fifty-two-year-old orca lives in captivity at the Miami Seaquarium in Florida. Tokitae is a Southern Resident orca too. Another orca, a Northern Resident living at SeaWorld San Diego, is about the same age as Tokitae. Scientists believe that in the wild, Northern Resident orcas live to be about sixty to eighty years old. Southern Resident whales, including Granny's J-pod, K-pod, and L-pod, seem to live longer. Lummi, the leader of K-pod, died at ninety-eight. Another head orca, Ocean Sun of L-pod, is going strong at eighty-seven. In December 2016, researchers reported that Granny, presumed to be the oldest-living Orca on Earth, had not been seen for several months and was presumed dead.

This photograph of the world's oldest-living whale, Granny, was taken in 2011 from Washington's Lime Kiln Point State Park. The park is on San Juan Island and is considered one of the best places in the world to see whales, especially orcas, from land.

The study of nature was also popular then, both among trained scientists and among average citizens. In fact, a new breed of scientist began studying animal behavior and physiology. Whales, so different from fish and other sea creatures, were of great interest.

As whales grew scarce toward the end of the nineteenth century, captains William Scoresby and C. M. Scammon, along with ship surgeons Thomas Beale and Frederick Debell Bennett, studied the situation closely. They learned more about where whales went during a year and when they might appear in any given location. They also observed the environmental lures, such as warm clear waters for birthing and cold rich waters for feeding, that attracted the animals to their favorite spots. This information added to the scientific knowledge of whales that would become the foundation of what we know today. And with better information, whalers could kill more whales, leading to further decimation of whale populations.

THE TWENTIETH-CENTURY WHALE

The Discovery Investigations, a decades-long British project to increase understanding of whale biology, began in 1925. The goal was to find out the diet and habitat whales needed to reproduce. At that time, whales were in danger of becoming extinct, and concerned conservationists wanted to be able to build up whale populations. The project centered on South Georgia Island, in the South Atlantic, a site where whalers brought their catch ashore for butchering. The Discovery scientists worked with these whalers, drawing on their knowledge of the health and habits of whales. Some researchers went to sea to learn about whale migration paths, traveling aboard the *Discovery.* This research ship had carried famous explorers Ernest Shackleton and Robert Falcon Scott to Antarctica in the early twentieth century.

Across the sea in London, England, the Natural History Museum commissioned the first realistic models of whales in the 1920s. The museum hired an engineer to make a mold of a dead whale. To do so, he would hang a dead blue whale by its tail in a graving dock, a space typically used for shipbuilding. To pay for the project, the museum planned to sell models cast from the mold to museums around the world. But the method didn't work. So the

Percy Stammwitz and his son Stuart were part of a team that built the famous 90-foot (27 m) model of a blue whale at the Natural History Museum in London. This photograph of the team with the wooden frame of the whale was taken in 1938.

museum's taxidermist (who preserves and stuffs dead animals for display), Percy Stammwitz, found a different way to build a blue whale model, using measurements from the scientists at South Georgia Island. He created his whale model using methods similar to those used to shape fighter planes. Starting with a wooden frame, Stammwitz overlaid it with wire mesh, then plaster. The model turned out to be an inaccurate version of the blue whale, but at the time, it was the best whale model ever made. And it inspired a new generation of whale watchers, many of whom would turn their attention to finding out more about live whales.

At about this time, Charles Haskins Townsend of the New York Zoological Society followed the lead of US naval officer Maury, using whalers' logs to map whales' breeding and mating grounds and their migration paths around the world. By then whaling had reached its crest. One hundred years later, whalers' logs are still useful. At the start of the twenty-first century, for example, Tim Smith and a group of scientists and historians working for the World Whaling History Project, part of the Census of Marine Life, delved into the logbooks again. They added to Maury's and Townsend's maps and data to create a database that, they estimated, represented 10 percent of American whaling voyages between 1780 and 1920—nearly fifteen hundred voyages. This gave the team a base plan to count the world's whales.

SAVING THE WHALES

On December 2, 1946, fifteen nations established the International Whaling Commission (IWC), based in Cambridge, England, to regulate the whaling industry. The primary goal is to ensure that whales are managed so that their numbers can recover from the decimation wreaked by commercial whaling. Nations that adopted the voluntary agreement to change their whaling practices to benefit whales included both whaling and non-whaling countries. Almost ninety nations are members. Most of them have undertaken a new approach to managing the whales in their waters. They first figured out what populations, or stocks of whales, lived in certain areas for at least part of a season and then worked to increase the health and well-being of those groups. Nations that signed on were allowed to continue to hunt whales for scientific reasons, but only if the meat was used for food.

In 1972 the United Nations Conference on the Human Environment recommended a temporary ten-year ban on whaling. In 1982 the IWC declared a moratorium (ban) on hunting whales, under which member nations were expected to end the practice entirely within four years. By then new scientific efforts were under way to understand just what percentage of previous whale stocks had been destroyed during the hundreds of years of heavy whaling.

Many species of whales were in danger of extinction, and with input from scientists, the conference determined that whale stocks needed a chance to recover. Whaling could continue legally only for scientific purposes or for subsistence hunting (in which the catch is used for food, not profit) by indigenous groups.

SAVE THE WHALES

Maris Sidenotecker was fourteen years old when she read about a pregnant blue whale that had died. So she designed a T-shirt with a blue whale on it, along with the words "Save the Whales," and used money from her savings account to print a dozen shirts and give them away. That was in 1975. So many people wanted the shirts that Maris began to sell them. By 1977 she had sold enough shirts to start a nonprofit organization called Save the Whales, the world's first whale conservation group.

Save the Whales became one of the great environmental movements of that decade. Whales became a symbol of a new understanding of the many ways that human activities can imperil the environment. Whales are a keystone species, whose health humans can look to as a sign of the health of the marine food chain and environment. The well-being of a whale symbolizes the care we give Mother Earth. The animal's distress or failing health is a sign of our poor treatment of our shared planet. Save the Whales focused on teaching young people about whales and publicizing conservation efforts. In the twenty-first century, the group helps publicize stories about people who have helped whales. Check out the "Heroes" section of the group's website.

EXCEPTIONS TO THE RULE

Norwegians followed the ban for a few years. But in 1993, Norway resumed hunting minke whales, setting its own quota (limit) of whales to one thousand a year. Since the moratorium is voluntary, the nation contended, Norway could opt out of it. Norway, therefore, continued to whale commercially.

In the mid-1990s, the IWC revisited the situation, using computer modeling to come up with a revised management plan (RMP). The goal was to figure out how many whales could be hunted from certain species while sustaining healthy population numbers. But the IWC members have never been able to agree on this RMP, so nothing has changed. Meanwhile, international organizations such as Sea Shepherd and Greenpeace actively oppose any whaling—so they are against the RMP. New IWC member countries include landlocked countries and others that support some whaling. This has shifted the members' opinion to a half-and-half split. It would take a 75 percent majority to lift the moratorium.

Some indigenous whalers preserve traditional hunting methods. These Iñupiat whalers, for example, prepare for a hunt in the Chuckchi Sea. They will go out in a skin boat with nonmechanized harpoons.

Among the indigenous groups allowed to whale under IWC guidelines are the Iñupiat in Alaska. Whaling is a vital part of their culture and their diet so they have the legal right to hunt bowhead and beluga whales. Iñupiat and other subsistence whale hunters are permitted to take a sustainable number of animals each year—that is, a small number that can be replenished through the animals' natural reproduction cycle. Whaling team captain Roy Ahmaogak, of Barrow, Alaska, says, "The whale gives itself, and we in turn pass on the gift." Indigenous whalers never hunt for profit. Some indigenous hunters are involved in scientific research with the goal of learning more about whales and preserving their environments for future generations of whales and people.

Meanwhile, increasing numbers of North Americans had begun to go out in boats—not to catch whales but to catch sight of them. The whale watching industry budded along whale migration routes in Canada, the United States, and Mexico. By 2008 whale watching boats were heading out from the shores of 119 countries, carrying nearly thirteen million whale watchers—and generating close to $1 billion in revenue each year.

WHALING WORLDWIDE

In the twenty-first century, three countries—Iceland, Japan, and Norway—continue to whale commercially. These nations take advantage of IWC scientific exemption loopholes, even in the face of an international outcry against their practices. They face no official sanctions (penalties).

Thanks to the ease of DNA testing and other high-tech methods, scientists only need to get small whale-tissue samples—or to capture whale exhalations or scoop up feces—to learn about the animal's physiology (physical health and functions). Therefore, most experts feel that whale hunting is not necessary to contribute to scientific understanding of these mammals. All the same, Iceland openly protests the IWC ban and continues to hunt whales, including endangered fin whales and minkes in the North Atlantic Ocean. The nation sells whale meat to Japan, supporting the commercial market for whale meat there. Like Iceland, Japan kills whales, saying it is to gain scientific specimens. Yet Japanese whalers sell the meat for cheap on the commercial market to build a big public demand for the meat.

Q:

How can you tell how old a whale is?

A:

If you saw the tooth of a toothed whale in half, you can count the rings on the inside of the tooth. Like a tree, one ring represents one year. With baleen whales, a DNA test is the best way to tell.

According to a 2014 Australian Broadcasting Corporation report, about thirty-two thousand whales have been legally killed since 1985—twenty thousand of them by Japanese whalers. Japan is the only nation that whales outside its own territory, in international waters. In 2014 Japan began a new program of whaling in Antarctica. And in 2015, the nation requested approval from individual members of the IWC for its plan to hunt minkes along its own coasts. The United States was among the many countries that refused to grant approval.

Gray whales, typically covered with barnacles, were hunted almost to extinction. They are now protected by international law. Some grays migrate more than 12,000 miles (20,000 km) round-trip from their summer habitat in Alaskan waters to the warmer waters off the Mexican coast. They mate and calve in Baja California, Mexico, where this photo was taken.

CHAPTER FOUR

SCHOOLING WITH WHALES

The public appetite for viewing cetaceans in the wild has become insatiable, growing itself to industrial scale.

—James Higham, Lars Bejder, and Rob Williams, *Whale-Watching: Sustainable Tourism and Ecological Management*, 2014

Humans have long looked out from shore to see whales spouting in the ocean. In the mid-twentieth century, commercial whaling was coming to an end and a new business—whale watching—was about to blossom. In 1957 whale watch boats in the United States first took tourists out into the Pacific Ocean from Southern California to see whales. The whales closest to shore were grays.

Whale watching helped support the conservation movement. As profits from recreational whale watching grew, whale watch captains wanted to ensure strong whale populations in their waters, and they began to cooperate with scientists to provide useful data. In 1967, for example, shore-based observers began keeping records of migrating eastern North Pacific gray whales from bluffs high above the sea. Gray whales are known for their friendliness and for the spinning, splashing mating games that draw whale watchers. The lagoons where they mate in Baja California are legally protected, and so are the whales.

Wayne Perryman, a California researcher at the Southwest Fisheries Science Center, is one of many whale conservationists who hope to achieve growing whale populations worldwide; increased data on whale health, habitat, and reproduction; and policies that protect the environment. He describes keeping count of gray whales in the early twenty-first century from a post at San Simeon, California. Over time, he noticed that the number of whale calves born in the calm waters of the coastal lagoons of Baja California, Mexico, had gone down. By also studying the gray whale feeding grounds—shallow areas in the Bering and Chukchi Seas to the north—scientists were able to link the low birth numbers with large amounts of ice in the northern waters. "Pregnant females are the first to return to the feeding grounds," Perryman said, piecing things together. "When the ice is slow to recede [melt back], their access to prey is impacted, and the likelihood that they'll have a calf the next year is reduced." (Scientists know that undernourished females have trouble becoming pregnant.)

THE FAMILY BUSINESS

Chad Avellar is a whale watch captain working in Provincetown, Massachusetts. His family emigrated from Portugal to Cape Cod long before Avellar was born. They came to work in the US fishing industry and were whale watch pioneers. Well into the 1970s, Avellar's grandfather, Al, made his living taking charter fishing groups into the ocean from Cape Cod. It was busy, grueling work. He got up early to track the fish, then went out to sea, baiting lines and teaching fishing. He coached clients as they reeled in their catches, and he helped with cleaning and filleting the catch. Finally, at day's end, he cleaned the boat and did laundry. Breaks came when whales passed by. "All the fishermen would stop what they were doing and just watch whales," Chad Avellar says. In the early 1970s, his grandfather had the idea of devoting one cruise a week to whale watching. He and a small crew would take visitors out to the fishing grounds at Stellwagen Bank National Marine Sanctuary, point out some of the whales that were almost always in the area, and return to port. It wasn't long before the whale watch cruises got so popular and were so much easier on the crew that the Avellars launched the Dolphin Fleet in 1975. It was the first whale watch business on the East Coast.

By the early 1990s, Dolphin Fleet was only one of many whale watch companies around the globe. In fact, with the growth in whale watch tours, the IWC formally recognized whale watching in 1993 as a legitimate tourism industry that allows for the sustainable use of whales.

During the 1990s, the number of people going on whale watches worldwide grew 12 percent a year. Between 1990 and 1999, for example, the International Fund for Animal Welfare (IFAW) reported that whale watching had expanded from two to nine million participants a year. By 2009 thirteen million people each year were enjoying whale watch cruises in 119 countries. The industry was earning more than $2.1 billion annually and employing thirteen thousand people. Whale watching is most popular in the United States. Close to five million people go to sea in the United States annually. That's 38 percent of all whale watchers worldwide. Among the countries where new whale watch businesses are launching are China, Cambodia, Nicaragua, and Panama.

Q:

Which whale swims the farthest?

A:

As scientists tag and track more whales via satellite, the record changes. For example, in 2007 a humpback mother and her calf went 5,160 miles (8,304 km). In 2015 the crown was taken by a tagged gray whale that traveled 14,000 miles (22,531 km) in 172 days.

DOWNSIDE TO WHALE WATCHING?

Before long, whale watchers had begun to swim in the water with cetaceans. Snorkelers approached sleeping dolphins, and scuba divers swam near to nursing mother humpbacks. People had fallen in love with up-close encounters, and in one sense, that seemed to be a good thing. Caring folks with personal experiences of whales would act to protect them and their waters. But what was good for whales, in general, did not always seem beneficial to individual whales.

In 2012 marine biologist E. C. M. Parsons of George Mason University in Virginia summarized the negative impacts of whale watching. He observed that whale watch boats change the way whales behave. For example, whales that are feeding when a whale watch boat nears might stop feeding or move

A diver in the Caribbean waters off the coast of the island nation of Dominica approaches a sperm whale. While many whales are friendly and seem to enjoy contact with humans, many experts agree that coming too close to a whale can stress the animal, even if we can't perceive it.

away from the boat. Nursing calves might get less food than they would without the boat in their mothers' feeding grounds. Whales that are resting or sleeping might wake or decide to move. And boats and whales in close proximity can lead to collisions between the animals and the boats. Boats also generate human and engine noise that can drown out sonar signals and other sounds that whales make to navigate or communicate. The noise can lead to wasted whale energy or to glitches in communication between whales. Parsons also noticed that some whales would abandon breeding grounds after they encountered whale watchers there. This displacement can stress whales in the same way moving from one house to another can stress humans.

THE BEST PRACTICES

Since whale watching as a tourist industry began, concerned citizens and scientists have wondered how to do it safely and respectfully. How close is too close for a boat to approach a whale? How many boats are too many in one area of the viewing area? International guidelines have laid out suggestions for how whale watch boats should behave around whales, but most of the suggestions (62 percent) are voluntary and unenforceable. Only 38 percent of the guidelines could actually lead to legal action.

Many whale watchers don't bother with the guidelines, even the ones that might lead to legal action. In each year of a study made between 1999 and 2002, two-thirds of human interactions with dolphins in one part of New Zealand, for example, violated the rule in the country's Marine Mammal Protection Act governing the number of swimmers that should be in the water near the dolphins. Certain dolphins do sometimes ride the bow waves of boats, but many go out of their way to avoid the boats' noise and pollution. And when snorkelers dive from tour boats to swim with dolphins, the animals will often make evasive moves to avoid the humans. Among the dolphins that are the most negatively impacted by tourists are the endangered Irrawaddy dolphins in the Mekong River on the Cambodia-Laos border.

Even with some regulations in place, enforcing them can be tough. And if it is hard to keep an eye on official whale watch operations, it is much harder to regulate private boaters. Many people disregard guidelines and go right up to whales, sometimes hitting them or disrupting their feeding and social behaviors. Whales in high-level whale watch areas are also exposed to diesel exhaust from boats and to other pollutants in the water. Whales will dive to get away, but increased lung pressure from diving may cause them to inhale even more of the pollutants.

Sometimes, however, curious whales will swim closer to humans. For example, this author was on a whale watch boat that a young humpback, out on his own for the first season, decided to investigate. He swam directly under the boat, with an intrigued expression in his eye as he gazed up at the whale watchers looking down at him, some of them reaching their hands toward him. The watchers felt changed for the better, wiser to the deeper workings of the world. Did he?

WHALE TO WATCH: AHWC NO. 1363

Humpback whales generally migrate north and south. They swim up to 5,000 miles (8,047 km) in their annual circuit between cold feeding grounds in polar waters and warm mating grounds in equatorial waters. So what would make a female humpback swim 6,200 miles (9,978 km) eastward? That's exactly what a whale, identified as Antarctic Humpback Whale Catalogue Number 1363—or AHWC No. 1363 for short—did from 1999 to 2001. The AHWC is an online source that provides photos and other information about individual whales from all over the world's oceans. Scientists use the resource to help identify and track specific whales.

Scientists were able to determine that AHWC No. 1363 had left her mating grounds along the coast of Brazil and, instead of shooting for her cold, southern feeding grounds, headed east, swimming all the way to Madagascar, an island nation off the southeastern coast of Africa. Researchers believe it is the longest trip ever made by a mammal (except humans). But they don't know why she did it. Marine ecologist Peter Stevick of the College of the Atlantic in Bar Harbor, Maine, wrote in *Biology Letters*, a British scientific journal published by the Royal Society, "It may be that this is an extreme example of exploration," he said. "Or it could be that the animal got very lost."

What's even more interesting is the way Stevick found out about the whale's trip. A colleague found a whale photo on a Norwegian tourist's Flickr site. That person, Freddy Johansen, had posted the image as a souvenir of a whale watching trip off the Madagascar coast in 2001. The colleague then went to the AHWC site to see if a match could be found. The catalogue photo that matched the whale in the tourist photo had been taken in 1999 on Abrolhos Bank, a group of islands along the Brazilian coast, confirming the whale's eastward journey.

The look of a whale's flukes is unique to that animal. The tail of AHWC No. 1363 has a distinct black-and-white pattern. She also has scars across her tail, the edge of which is very jagged.

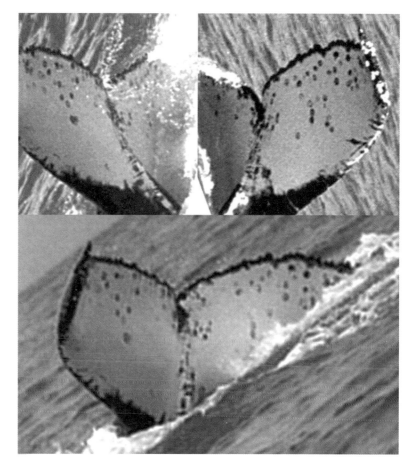

Parsons has concluded that even though whale watching is satisfying for humans, it is something that does not benefit whales overall. He says, "One simple method for reducing the impacts of whale watching is to establish refuges; that is, no-go or sanctuary areas. Ideally such areas would allow animals to engage in biologically important behaviors (feeding, resting, or nursing) without being disturbed by whale watching vessels."

CHAPTER FIVE

WHAT DO CETOLOGISTS DO?

Mike Bursk is the captain of *Sea Explorer*, a Dana Point Ocean Institute research vessel in Southern California. He has been watching whales for thirty years. In 2014 Bursk was among the first to spot a pod of false killer whales off the coast of Dana Point. The sighting in this part of the Pacific Ocean is rare because the animals usually prefer warmer waters near the Hawaiian islands.

The source of any conflict in the industry of whale watching has been, Are we loving them to death? We created a campaign with the slogan "Don't be the fifth boat" to help establish this rule of thumb: if you come up and there are already four boats [near a whale], five is too many.

—Sarah Wilson Finstuen, whale watch naturalist, 2015

Since the 1970s, Roger Payne of Ocean Alliance, an organization dedicated to whale and marine conservation, has worked to become an expert on the South Atlantic right whales that live just off a beach in Patagonia, along the Atlantic coast of Argentina. To track whales from atop a cliff, Payne began using a theodolite, an instrument that land surveyors rely on when making maps. The theodolite would help Payne find out how far away whales were. When Payne noticed that whales didn't react to planes flying low overhead, he began doing aerial surveys and added new observation data from his flyovers. Besides learning more about whales, he spread the word to other scientists about his innovative ways of finding information. They followed suit in their own studies.

Scientists who watch whales don't just observe. They work to establish situational awareness—a picture of a whale's entire life. Researchers work to develop technologies and methods for learning where whales are, which individual whales are there, and what they're doing. Are they eating? Mating? Calving? Migrating? Cetologists also assess the state of the waters where the whales are living. One of the greatest challenges of whale research is to evaluate and understand the impact of human influences: noise and water pollution, trends in water temperature or chemistry due to climate change, and the perils of fishing gear and other trash.

Scientists doing whale research are in a race to gather data. Why the big rush? Environmental stresses are changing quickly, and scientific understanding of whale habitat could impact laws and policies that might slow or

Q:

Which whale has the biggest brain?

A:

With an average weight of 17 pounds (7.8 kilograms), the sperm whale brain is the heaviest brain of all whale brains—and the heaviest on the planet.

alter changes to habitat. For instance, reduced ice levels in the Arctic Ocean due to global warming have opened up new commercial shipping lanes. So whales that have never encountered large ships in these waters will likely do so. Scientists want a clear picture of the conditions in which whales flourished before ice loss. That way we can better address whale needs as their Arctic homelands become increasingly impacted by human shipping.

MONITORING FEEDING AND FATNESS

Two key indicators of whale health are feeding and fatness. In *Voices in the Sea*, an online multimedia exhibit, biologist Wayne Perryman describes taking pictures of whales from planes. He wanted to measure how fat or thin gray whales were as they passed through the ocean waters of Southern California on the way south from their northern feeding grounds. Perryman understands that whales' waistlines naturally narrow during this migratory period because the animals do not eat as often as they do in their food-rich northern waters. He learned that whales were thinner in some seasons than others, depending on how much food was available. Perryman also knows that if food resources are too scarce, whales die. In some seasons, he did observe larger numbers of dead whales. In recent research, Perryman is among the many scientists who have realized that climate change is affecting the food supply. With waters warming worldwide, some whale food sources are more plentiful in some places and are therefore drawing whales to areas where they used to be scarcer.

Other research focuses on the Arctic Ocean, which is shallower than the world's other oceans. Gray whales burrow into the sediment on the Arctic

Gray whales, such as this one off the Pacific coast of British Columbia in western Canada, feed by stirring up the sediments on the bottom of the ocean. They then filter out the fish that come up with the sediments. Cetologists want to fully understand a whale's feeding patterns as part of establishing situational awareness of that animal's life.

seafloor to sift fish and other food from the mud. As they feed, the whales churn up the sediment. It settles into beds in which organisms such as amphipods (a crustacean) can grow. Scientists think that with climate change more whales are likely to live in the Arctic Ocean. Cetologists want to know how changes in the whale population might affect this environment.

The Center for Coastal Studies (CCS) in Provincetown, Massachusetts, continually monitors the levels of whale food in Cape Cod Bay, an arm of the Atlantic. Whales that come here to feed on zooplankton include right whales, humpbacks, minke, fin whales and, once in a blue moon, a blue whale. The cold water welling up from the bottom of the Atlantic Ocean here sustains the life the whales depend on. But as temperatures rise due to climate change, ocean temperatures rise too. The plankton in the bay could be forced northward in search of the colder waters they prefer. Whales would therefore have fewer food sources in this part of the ocean.

Scientists are dedicated to understanding the ways that groups of whales

Cetaceans work together to hunt for food. Groups of dolphins, for example, corral sardines and other small fish for food. These dolphins are feeding in the Indian Ocean, off the southeastern coast of South Africa.

feed. Humpbacks work together to blow bubbles that create a water net to herd prey fish toward the surface, where the whales will scoop them up. In the waters of the northern Pacific, orcas practice carousel feeding, working in a team to corral (gather) prey. The orcas then take turns darting into the center to grab fish. Dolphins off the coast of Florida build a horseshoe shape in the sand of the seafloor, and they work together to herd fish into this "net." By observing how and what whales and dolphins eat, and by comparing this information to the animals' weight and health, scientists get a sense of what's normal for them. This is the first step in troubleshooting when something is different or goes wrong.

GETTING TO KNOW INDIVIDUAL HUMPBACKS

One way cetologists study whale health is by getting to recognize and know individual whales. Jooke Robbins of the University of Massachusetts, Boston, is the director of humpback whale research at the CCS. The center is the home of the Avellar family's Dolphin Fleet. The CCS, founded in 1976, grew up alongside the fleet.

"It's only been in the lifetime of adults [of the early twenty-first century] that humpback whales and other marine mammals have been studied based on their natural markings," Robbins says. Doing so helps scientists see whales as individuals, and from that, they can see what differentiates each whale from the next one. By identifying them, they've begun thinking of whales completely differently.

"Just the idea of naming them has a lot of power," Robbins continues. "Each time someone sees [a whale] they're adding to knowledge about [that whale]. For scientists it means that we can understand the things that happen to the whale and how it has been living since the last time we saw it."

Identifying and tracking individual whales started with another CCS scientist named Charles "Stormy" Mayo, the descendant of a whaling family that stepped ashore on Cape Cod in 1650. Mayo was aboard the whale watch boat of Aaron Avellar (Chad Avellar's father) in 1975 when the crew noticed a humpback whale with unique coloration on her back. She had a dorsal fin that looked as if it was encrusted with salt, so Avellar named the whale Salt. He named her companion whale Pepper.

The first whale catalogue launched in 1977, when researchers from Allied Whale at the College of the Atlantic in Maine began to organize, compare, and categorize pictures of 120 whale tails. The catalogue included Mayo's photograph of Salt's distinctive tail. (Salt is also known as Humpback Whale Catalogue [HWC] #0036.) The catalogue has grown to include photos of more than eight thousand individual humpbacks. The humpback research program at the CCS relies on the whale catalogue to identify and track individual whales. By studying the catalogue, cetologists realized that Atlantic humpbacks summer in the Gulf of Maine and swim south to the Caribbean Sea in the fall to mate and give birth. It is one of the longest migration loops of any mammal, with a round-trip of up to 8,000 miles (12,875 km).

In 1981 Allied Whale began building a catalogue of North Atlantic finback whales that has since grown to eight hundred whales. These North American whale catalogues have inspired scientists to launch catalogues for other whale populations, oceans, and regions, including Antarctica.

In the twenty-first century, Salt sightings are celebrated by whale watchers who have known the humpback for years. No one greets her with more enthusiasm than Chad Avellar. Aaron Avellar and his family have the privilege of naming her

WHALE TO WATCH: SALT

During the 2015 calving season, Salt became a mother, a grandmother, and a great-grandmother. Since the mid-1970s, this "very special whale" has been spotted seasonally in the Gulf of Maine and also in her winter grounds in the Caribbean, where she goes to mate and have calves.

Identifying and naming Salt was a game changer for researchers seeking a better understanding of the lives of whales. The ability to recognize whales meant that they could track their migrations. What's more, they could trace their family trees. Genetic (DNA) analysis of tissue samples from Salt and her calves led to the realization that female whales mate with different males from season to season. Their calves therefore have different fathers. This helps ensure a strong genetic pool among each generation of whales.

When scientists were able to sequence the entire genome of the humpback whale, in the early 1990s, guess who they chose? Salt! Her DNA represents the humpback genome, giving scientists insight into how her genes direct the growth and development of a humpback whale.

calves—all fourteen of them. As of 2016, Salt has fifteen grandchildren—and even two great-grandchildren, born to Salt's granddaughter Etch-a-Sketch.

A WORLD OF MIGRATING WHALES

In the summers of 1992 and 1993, an international group of scientists did research for the Years of the North Atlantic Humpback (YoNAH) project. Their aim was to identify and map the migratory paths of humpback whales all over the North Atlantic Ocean. What they learned changed their understanding of whale populations, migrations, and behaviors. The accepted wisdom had been that whales feeding off the coast of Norway in summer went south to mate in the warmer Atlantic waters off the Cape Verde islands. The YoNAH whale count of humpbacks that mated and calved in the Caribbean Sea, far to Norway's west, was 10,572 whales in 1993. This number wasn't that much lower than the total number of humpbacks in the North Atlantic—about 11,570. This indicated to scientists that the Norwegian humpbacks were likely heading west rather than south to mate. What's more, scientists noticed that North Atlantic humpbacks in different parts of the Atlantic Ocean were swimming to the Caribbean on different schedules, reaching the mating and breeding grounds at different times. With differing numbers of whales in the breeding grounds, this meant that some whales had a better chance of mating than others.

Ten years later, scientists working on the More North Atlantic Humpback (MoNAH) whales project conducted research from 2003 to 2005. Their goal was to learn more about the whales that migrate annually between Stellwagen Bank, in the Gulf of Maine, and Silver Bank, 60 miles (97 km) north of the Dominican Republic in the Caribbean. They learned that humpbacks are loyal to their feeding grounds in summer, returning to the same places and to the same whales every year. Yet when they are in the southern mating grounds, they mix it up with whales from different feeding aggregations (groups). Scientists think this mating behavior may indicate that whales naturally ensure a diverse, strong gene pool by avoiding repeat mating with the same whales every year.

Another humpback study focuses on Pacific whales. The Structure of Populations, Levels of Abundance, and Status of Humpbacks (SPLASH) program is one of the world's largest collaborations of international scientists. More than four hundred researchers from ten countries are seeking an understanding of humpback populations in the Northern Pacific and the impact of human activities on them.

Worldwide, researchers are looking for as much information as possible about every whale in the planet's oceans. Whale by whale, counting and identifications of individuals and their behaviors help researchers understand how whales use feeding and mating opportunities, ocean depths, the sea bottom, sea temperature, and other marine factors. In this way, cetologists gain an understanding of how the ocean works for whales. They can then make more informed suggestions for how to manage the seas to ensure the long-term survival of whales.

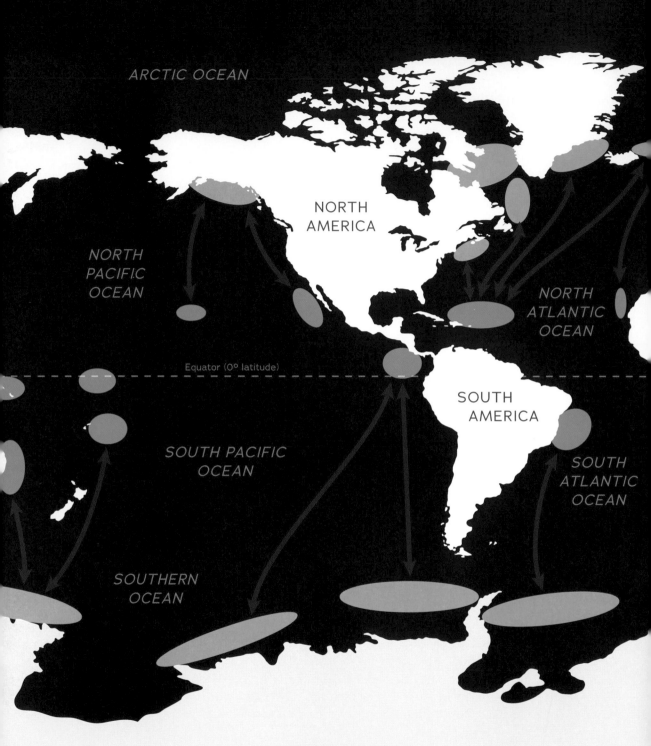

ARCTIC OCEAN

NORTH
AMERICA

NORTH
PACIFIC
OCEAN

NORTH
ATLANTIC
OCEAN

Equator (0° latitude)

SOUTH
AMERICA

SOUTH PACIFIC
OCEAN

SOUTH
ATLANTIC
OCEAN

SOUTHERN
OCEAN

ANTARCTICA

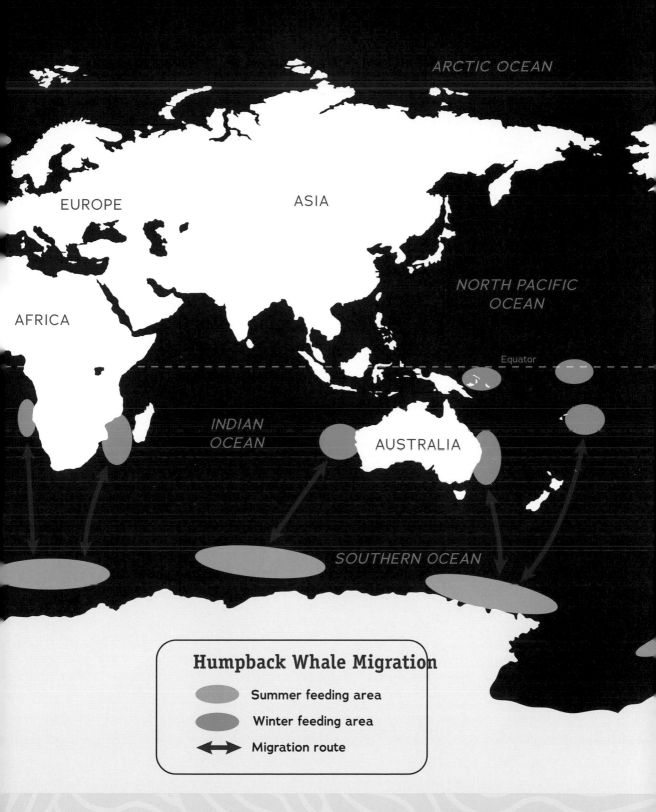

ARCTIC OCEAN

EUROPE

ASIA

AFRICA

NORTH PACIFIC
OCEAN

Equator

INDIAN
OCEAN

AUSTRALIA

SOUTHERN OCEAN

Humpback Whale Migration

- Summer feeding area
- Winter feeding area
- ↔ Migration route

CHAPTER SIX

LISTENING FOR WHALES

A curious humpback whale approaches a hydrophone dangling from a research vessel off the coast of Maui, Hawaii. Researchers use these recording devices to capture the sounds of the ocean, including whale calls. Humpback songs are the most creative in the cetacean world. They make a wide range of calls, including grunts, groans, and bark-like calls. Their songs fall within the widest Hertz range of any whale, from twenty to eighteen hundred vibrations per second. (One hertz is one sound wave cycle per second.)

They sound like jaguars and horses,
and sometimes how I imagine mermaids
and ghosts might sound.

—Michelle Fournet, Oregon State University graduate student,
about the sound of whale vocalization, 2014

The sea is not a silent place. Waves break, underwater earthquakes rumble, wind shakes the surface, and lightning strikes it with a sizzle. Sea creatures are anything but mute. Shrimp snap, fish croak, and whales chirp, cheep, and groan, echoing from the seabed to the sky and reverberating from one side of an ocean basin to the other. The finback's call is so deep in tone that scientists who first heard it thought the seafloor itself was creaking.

The blue whale's call is the loudest in the ocean, yet humans can't hear it at all. Its frequency, or pitch (the number of oscillations—waves or cycles—the whale's sound makes), is 14 hertz, well below human hearing range. (Humans hear pitches in the 20-hertz range.) We can hear a blue whale's clicks and blows, and we can feel the vibration of its call, but we can't hear the tone of the call itself. At 180 decibels (the measurement of how loud a note is), the call could blow our eardrums out—if we could hear it in the first place.

The sperm whale—the deepest diver—seems to define its world through sound, not sight. Cetologists think other whales probably do too. In his book *The Whale*, Philip Hoare described the sperm whale as having the world's largest sound system. The animal uses one-third of its body to produce clicks and to amplify their sound so that it spreads out for miles, then echoes off walls or fish. This gives the whale an acoustic image of its surroundings. Whales communicate in sonar pulses, rhythmic sound waves that bounce and amplify along layers of water to help whales stay in contact across hundreds of miles.

Seawater isn't uniform. It has different depths, temperatures, chemistry, pressure levels, and other properties. In the sea, sound travels fastest and farthest along what scientists call the Sound Fixing and Ranging (SOFAR) channel. This channel is a horizontal layer of ocean water where low-frequency sounds—such as whale calls—can travel the farthest. The channel is at different depths in different parts of the world's oceans. For example, off the coast of Bermuda in the Caribbean, the SOFAR channel is at a depth of 3,281 feet (1,000 m). Whales seek the channel and use it to communicate across the ocean.

BEST NEW ARTIST

In 1970 biologist Roger Payne cut a record with the music of a new, just-discovered talent: humpback whales. When his recording of North Pacific humpbacks came out, it won the hearts of the American public and intrigued a new generation of marine biologists. With the sale of one hundred thousand records, the album, *Songs of the Humpback Whale*, is still the biggest-selling natural history recording ever. "At the time, whales were being killed to the tune of 33,000 a year," Payne said in the documentary film *Voices of the Sea*. "When people could hear these beautiful sounds, it became harder to think of turning these animals into lipstick and shoe polish and cat food and all of the things which they were being turned into at that time."

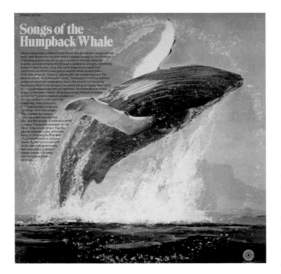

Roger Payne's 1970 album *Songs of the Humpback Whale* was inducted into the National Recording Registry, a Library of Congress list of recordings that are considered culturally and historically important to Americans.

Humpbacks seem to share vocal passwords with one another through song. They announce their membership in the pod and teach one another new variations to their tune. They cover thousands of miles a year, often traveling out of sight of one another yet staying in touch vocally.

People listening to the recording of the humpbacks' singing didn't know how the whales made noise, who or what the sounds were for, or what the songs meant (if anything). But the sound—spooky, guttural, glorious—touched listeners. They responded as if the whales were sending humans a message, and they leaned in, wanting to know more. The sounds whales made inspired vital new areas of research.

FOLLOWING THE NOTES

One goal of acoustic research is to locate whales. Another is to figure out the meaning of whale sounds. Cetologists also want to know how whales use their lungs and skulls and other attributes to generate noise that can carry across hundreds of miles of ocean.

Another goal is to figure out why whales vocalize. Payne realized that humpbacks weren't just making noise, they were singing songs. For example, scientists know that birds use song to communicate in mating, territorial defense, declaration of membership in the group, and for other reasons. This led Payne to think that whales too have messages to share. "There are anywhere between two and nine themes that come into the humpback's song, and each theme is divided into anywhere up to 15 or 20 different repetitions of a phrase," he says. Whale songs are much longer than bird songs, averaging between five and thirty minutes. "They make a continual river of sound that can go for as long as . . . 36 hours without stopping." To sing without interrupting themselves with breaths at the surface, Payne felt, the whales had to be consciously performing.

Because birds and other animals sing or call for mates, scientists assumed that humpbacks were doing this too. But biologist Jim Darling of the Whale Trust, an organization involved in science research and public education, says scientists have never actually observed this in action. "All the evidence we have is that this is an interaction or signal between males." He said that when two singing males meet, the singing stops, then the males split, heading in different directions—often toward females. "Why do they sing?" Darling asks. "We have a ways to go with that question."

Ellen Garland, a doctoral student at the University of Queensland in Australia, studies whale vocalizations. In 2011 she published humpback song

HOW DO WHALES HEAR?

For a mammal to hear, sound must travel to a part of the ear called the inner, or middle, ear. In odontocetes, the outer ear is plugged with wax, so sound travels to the middle ear through ligaments in the jaw. Scientists aren't sure how mysticetes hear. These whales have ear bones that connect to their skulls and that could carry sound vibrations to the middle ear. Researchers are working to understand how these whales receive sound.

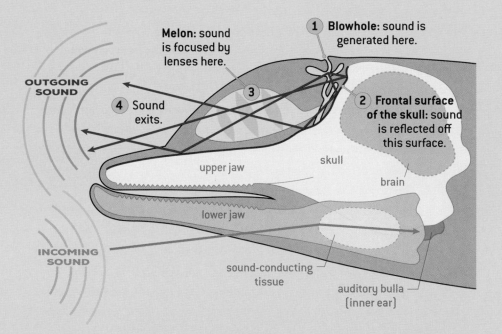

CETACEAN ECHOLOCATION

research that represented scientists' observations from all over the world. She compares the spread of humpback song through the water to ripples in the ocean. Song passes from one group of whales to another and, like a rumor, shifts over time in a cycle. As a song spreads, whales will change notes and rhythms of their tune. This was the first time a scientist had traced whale song around the world—a moving, changing story-message as real and traceable as a Facebook meme.

SOUNDING OUT POLAR WHALES

Autonomous gliders are robots that go to sea instead of scientists. Mark Baumgartner, a biologist at Woods Hole Oceanographic Institution, uses gliders to gather whale sound. They also help him learn more about how whales live in their environment and where they are migrating. Seasickness in stormy seas motivated Baumgartner to find a new way to gather data in whale habitat. A ship can put the gliders in the water, then return to shore where scientists await communications relayed back to their computers. A Slocum glider uses a buoyancy pump to move up and down in the water column to get deep enough to record whale sounds. A new glider called a wave glider has batteries that get juiced by a combination of wave energy and solar power to dive deep.

As a glider dives, sensors gather information about the sea's temperature and salinity (amount of salt in the water). A microphone picks up sounds from the surrounding area, and a computer matches sounds with whale calls from a digital call library. The glider surfaces and zaps its data to an Iridium satellite, which then relays the data to onshore computers.

In 2013 Baumgartner and his research partners Kate Stafford of the University of Washington and Peter Winsor of the University of Alaska at Fairbanks began a glider project in the Chukchi Sea, off the northwestern coast of Alaska. Their goal was to monitor the impact of climate change on marine mammals. "Climate change is happening in the Arctic. We want to do this survey every year for many years, to see how the ocean changes and to see how marine mammals change their distribution," Baumgartner says. "Subarctic species, namely humpbacks and finback whales, were rarely seen in this region before, but now we're seeing more and more of them (as the ocean warms)."

WHALE TO WATCH: THE 52 HERTZ WHALE

US Navy hydrophones picked up the songs of a lone blue whale in the North Pacific Ocean in 1989. But something was weird about the whale's song. It was singing in a voice at a frequency of 52 hertz, well above the normal 10- to 40-hertz range of other blue whales. No other whales responded to this unusual voice, suggesting that the whale—known as the 52 Hertz whale—was a pariah, isolated from whale social groups.

Bill Watkins of WHOI had studied whale songs of unusual frequency for many years. In 2004 he published a paper about his unusual study. In the paper, Watkins insisted that only one whale call had ever been found at this frequency.

Scientist Christopher Willes Clark of Cornell University in New York has suggested that this whale might be using a dialect—a regional adaptation of the song. Dialects are not unheard of among humpbacks and other singing whales. "The animal's singing with a lot of the same features of a typical blue whale song," he told the British Broadcasting Corporation. "Blue whales, fin whales and humpback whales: all these whales can hear this guy, they're not deaf. He's just odd."

Something else has caught the attention of cetologists. The 52 Hertz whale has lowered his tone. As he grows older, his voice changes. By 2015 he was singing at about 47 hertz, closer to normal range. What's more, he's not the only one to do so. Worldwide, blue whale voices have been deepening. This may be a natural occurrence as the whales gain weight and grow older.

New acoustic technology aids research in the Antarctic Ocean too. Scientists with the Alfred Wegener Institute installed the Perennial Acoustic Observatory in the Antarctic Ocean (PALAOA) in 2005. (The word *palaoa* means "whale" in Hawaiian.) They drilled holes in ice 329 feet (100 m) thick near the German polar research Neumayer Station III in Antarctica. They placed a network of hydrophones and other sensors into the water through the holes. PALAOA equipment continually records under-the-ice sounds along a wide range of frequencies. It can pick up everything from the lowest tones of big blue whales (10 hertz) to the higher clicks of orcas (20 to 70 hertz). Among the cetacean surprises? Humpback whales and blue whales, previously believed to stay out of ice-covered waters, come south to Antarctica, even in the polar winter.

What's more, PALAOA sound tracks have been incorporated into artwork to reach the ears of a wider public. In 2010 about three million people visited an art installation floating on the Ruhr River in the German city of Essen. It combined sculptures of icebergs, ships, and oil platforms as well as whale sounds to bring the audience closer to features of the marine environment, including Antarctic whales.

Singing for Their Supper

Whales have no vocal cords—the folds of tissue humans and most mammals use to vocalize (talk or call). The sperm whale produces sonar clicks that echo through the water to help detect prey. To make these clicks, the whale feeds air from its lungs through its nasal passages and a valve called phonic lips, or the

This floating sculpture of an iceberg was part of a 2010 exhibit in the Ruhr River in Germany. The sculpture played the PALAOA recordings of under-the-ice sounds.

ANTARCTIC BLUE WHALE SONG

Antarctic blue whales were hunted almost to extinction. But they are surviving, and in the twenty-first century, the IWC has located about three hundred of the whales. Their sounds are infrasonic, which means they make vibrations that humans can sometimes feel but not hear. The whale's highest pitch is only 86 hertz.

In 2015 Brian Miller, an acoustician (sound specialist) with the Australian Antarctic Division, deployed a floating array of microphones called a sonobuoy from a research ship. He then made the first recording of the Antarctic blue whale's song. Back ashore, he used a computer to raise the song 10 semitones—about two octaves above the whales' regular pitch. He began to feel its vibrations at this higher pitch. Raising it 20 semitones put it into human hearing range, the first time a human has ever been able to hear the song of an Antarctic blue whale.

monkey's muzzle (this makes the cracking click sound). The air then passes through a large oil-filled organ in the skull called the junk (the dome-shaped portion of the skull), where the sound is amplified and directed.

Sonar echoes from dolphins and from toothed whales such as sperm whales. It bounces back to help them locate and size up prey. Underwater photographer Howard Hall describes the whale sounds he experienced while making the MacGillivray Freeman *Humpback Whales* documentary. "It's very low frequency so it goes directly to your middle ear and pulses go right through your body tissues. The vibrations are so strong you can actually feel the air vibrating in your lungs."

Sperm whales also make booming sounds that some scientists think may be used to stun or actually kill prey. For example, some researchers think the sound may shock plankton in the deep so much that they bioluminesce (light up). The whale can then track the light to find—and eat—the plankton.

Cetaceans use sound to check out mates, evaluate competitors, and identify themselves to other whales. Baleen whales such as humpbacks and fin whales make their sounds differently than toothed whales do. Instead of phonic lips, they have a larynx, as humans do, but not vocal cords. Experts aren't sure exactly how baleen whales form sound, but they do know that like toothed whales, they use sounds to communicate, assess other whales, and find food. These whales don't chase down their prey individually as toothed whales do. Instead, they use sound to organize one another into teams for rounding up and capturing prey to filter through their baleen. Humpbacks coordinate their moves in unison—not unlike synchronized swimmers—to shape bubble nets, herd prey, and lunge up through the water to feed.

LEND ME YOUR EARS

Who's an expert on distinguishing between voices, tones of voice, and vocal messages? You might be. When Oregon State University graduate student Michelle Fournet wanted to analyze hundreds of whale calls, she enlisted the help of listeners who communicate vocally all the time—people!

Whales use sound to communicate, and they often work together to hunt prey. This humpback, for example, works with other whales to blow bubbles beneath a school of fish. The column of bubbles surrounds the fish and forces them upward. The whales—mouths open—swim up and through the bubble net. They catch thousands of fish in one mouthful.

"Humans are champion acoustic discriminators," she says. Her research project involves having people listen to and analyze hundreds of whale calls.

Through the Alaska Whale Foundation (AWF), Fournet invited volunteers—citizen scientists—to listen to whale calls that hydrophones on buoys or nearby boats picked up. The volunteers detected subtle differences among vocalizations and classified them into different call types. Under the leadership of biologist Fred Sharpe, the AWF has been collecting entries for a new kind of humpback catalogue since the 1990s. This will be a catalogue of vocalizations that humpback whales make in their foraging (feeding) grounds.

The next step is to understand how the vocalizations correspond to what the whales are doing as they forage for food. Volunteers are watching whales from the Five Fingers Lighthouse in Frederick Sound, Alaska. They are looking for specific behaviors and social patterns—such as which whale is with which other whale—to correlate, or match, with specific vocalizations the whales make.

Making these correlations will help scientists know what whales are saying. But the AWF has another goal: "We hope to use this information to anticipate some of the consequences humpbacks will face as ocean noise [from ships and their sonar systems] continues to rise."

THE TROUBLE WITH SONAR

In 2000 the US Navy conducted sonar testing in the Bahamas as part of military tracking exercises. Afterward, rescue organizations answered calls about whales of four different species found dead, dying, and stranding (swimming into shore and getting stuck in the shallows) on nearby beaches. Necropsies (physical exams of animals after death) revealed bleeding lesions in whales' ears and even around vital organs such as kidneys, liver, and lungs. These lesions are symptoms of the bends, a life-threatening condition caused by swimming up too quickly to the water's surface from deep below. Scientists wondered if the whales were getting the bends from moving too quickly upward in the water to flee the noise of sonar testing. They worried that seismic testing (guns that crews fire from a ship into the bottom of the ocean to analyze sediments there) posed the same threat.

What level of noise might cause whales to flee rapidly? As a ship sends out sonar, sound levels are like "rolling walls of noise," reaching 235 decibels—

twice the level of the loudest rock band   according to *Scientific American*.
Scientists have evidence that sonar has the potential to harm, alarm, or
disorient whales. The noise of seismic guns does too. They both seem to
coincide with beaching whales.

The Natural Resources Defense Council and several other environmental
organizations brought a lawsuit against the US Navy for conducting tests off the
coasts of Hawaii and California. In 2015 a federal court ruled that the military
testing of powerful sonar and explosive seismic guns violated the US Marine
Mammal Protection Act and the Endangered Species Act. The US Navy faced
losing the ability to train and test systems they feel are critical to national
security. As a compromise, the US Navy chose to stop training and testing only
in "biologically significant areas." These areas are in coastal waters that are vital
to whales, dolphins, seals, and sea lions.

CHAPTER SEVEN
FROM SNOTBOTS
TO
FECES FINDERS

Operators on the exploration research vessel *Nautilus* pull up *Hercules*, an underwater remotely operated vehicle. The ROV can dive as deep as 2.5 miles (4,023 m). It carries cameras and acoustic sensors to gather video and other data about whales and other marine life.

Our future problem is surveying [whales] and assessing stock [counting and understanding them]. We need to detect changes in populations in time to protect them.

—Peter Tyack, University of Saint Andrews, Scotland, speaking to the Society for Marine Mammalogy, 2015

Between 1982 and 2015, scientists worked with various techniques to watch whales in their natural environments. For example, a film crew from the United States went to Trincomalee, Sri Lanka. There, in 1982, they shot the first underwater film of sperm whales. The crew was part of the research vessel *Tulip*. Marine biologist Hal Whitehead led the vessel's research team to do the world's first study of sperm whales. The groundbreaking footage was featured in a 1983 American documentary called *Whales Weep Not*.

But who knew that whales would be watching us too? *Hercules* is an underwater remotely operated vehicle (ROV)—a robot submarine. It operates deep in the water, tethered to its mother ship, Exploration Vessel *Nautilus*. During a 2015 deep-sea research dive 1,962 feet (598 m) deep in the Gulf of Mexico, *Hercules* had a surprise visitor. A dark, square shadow suddenly loomed from the murky seafloor. Hoots and hollers erupted from the team watching from aboard *Nautilus* through the ROV's cameras. For nearly twenty minutes, a young male sperm whale emerged from the gloom to check out *Hercules*. The whale swam around eyeballing the vehicle. A worldwide audience watched the camera feed on laptop computers and smartphones. It was a moment to hang a star on—a firsthand look at a whale in its natural environment.

PIGGYBACK PHOTOGRAPHY

In 1986, about forty years before the *Hercules* encounter, University of Maryland scientist Greg Marshall invented Crittercam. This small package of instruments includes a video camera that attaches to an animal for a limited time. To deploy a Crittercam on a whale, a technician uses a pole to attach a suction cup onto the whale's back. The suction cup is attached to a small video camera the size and shape of a cucumber.

The 2004 test ride for Crittercam was on short-finned pilot whales off the coast of Kona, Hawaii. Researchers wanted to know what kept this population of pilot whales hugging the sharp cliff of a seamount (underwater volcano) along the coast of the Big Island of Hawaii. Crittercam videos and depth measurements revealed that pilot whales there feed in different ways than those in European waters. Scientists wonder if it is because the Hawaiian waters are clearer. And the video footage showed what, when, and how these whales hunted.

In another Crittercam project, in 2008, humpback whales gave a demonstration for the camera of how they create the bubble net they use to trap herring. AWF biologist Fred Sharpe had been studying the same pod of humpbacks in Chatham Strait in southern Alaska for fifteen years. He has studied the bubble net feeding for even longer. The 2008 video gave him a new perspective—a whale's-eye view.

The video helped Sharpe see how the whales use teamwork. "You've got some [whales] that blow the bubbles, others that go down and herd the prey toward the surface, and other individuals that scream these incredibly beautiful and haunting songs to clump the prey up and force them up toward the surface into the confines of the bubble net," he said. Sharpe was able to observe how the whales organize. "They all get together in the group and they come charging up through this tunnel of bubbles almost like missiles coming up through a [military] silo. They engulf the prey in their huge mouths at the surface."

GoPro cameras have also been a game changer for whale watchers and scientists. Before scientists had underwater technology, researchers could only work with what they could see from above the surface of the ocean. With a GoPro on a stick, scientists can dip cameras under the surface to get a whale's-eye view.

WHALES FROM THE SKY

Frances Robertson is a wildlife biologist at the University of British Columbia, Canada. She studies the impacts on minke whales of sound, gas and oil exploration, and the presence of large vessels in the whales' Salish Sea habitat.

Researchers like Robertson make aerial surveys with cameras carried by researchers flying in small planes. These surveys help paint a picture of whale distribution (how widespread or concentrated they are) in an area. They also help scientists learn about the abundance of whales (how many there are) in any one area. Aerial surveyors gather data and do a little math. This helps them make educated guesses about the total number of whales that might have been diving when the planes flew over. But aerial surveys have drawbacks. Hiring a crew and paying for fuel are expensive. And the planes must fly relatively low to see the whales. So pilots and crew face additional risks when they fly at lower altitudes because they can't afford to make mistakes this close to the water. Robertson also uses a less expensive land-based camera-tracking system to follow harbor porpoises to see how they respond to noise generated by tidal turbine devices. These machines use the ebb and flow of ocean tides to generate electricity.

SPOTLIGHT ON DRONES

Battery-operated drones, or unmanned aerial vehicles (UAVs), are a useful tool for studying whale health. A team of scientists from Vancouver Aquarium in British Columbia and NOAA's National Marine Fisheries Service (NMFS) have been using drone photography since 2014. They want to determine if killer whales in the northern Pacific are skinny or fat and also whether females are pregnant. Determining if whales are pregnant allows scientists to estimate calving rates (how often females have calves). It also helps them figure out calf success rates (how many newborn whales live after birth). These are key factors for understanding the health of a whale population.

John Durban of the National Marine Fisheries Service took a research boat into the San Juan Islands off the northwestern coast of the United States. There, he deployed the Hexacopter, a drone camera. The Hexacopter flies much lower than the helicopters or planes that scientists often use, so they can take images that are amazingly clear. The Hexacopter's altimeter (instrument that measures altitude) and camera also provide photogrammetry options. With these options, scientists then can measure a whale's length and girth (waistline). The data helps researchers understand how robust (healthy, from eating good food) a whale is.

WHALE TO WATCH: L-122

Orca L-122 was just days old when the Hexacopter drone buzzed over his head and took his picture. Born in 2015, L-122 was one of five calves of the Southern Resident killer whales that live in Puget Sound, off the San Juan Islands. With his birth, his pod's population rose to eighty-one whales. Scientists are carefully studying this group—a NOAA Species in the Spotlight—to find out what it requires to thrive.

"This is the smallest calf we've ever photographed from the air," scientist John Durban of NMFS told Rich Press of NOAA. "I think what I love . . . is the kind of nurturing you see [in the picture]. The calf is swimming up by its mother's head . . . by her eyes. She's keeping an eye on it. That just shows you the level of care and close nurturing that's going to go on and really [continue] through this calf's life. Its mom is its ticket to growing and making it, and it's great to see this close bond in the early days of life." The research group hopes to continue monitoring L-122 with the help of Hexacopter.

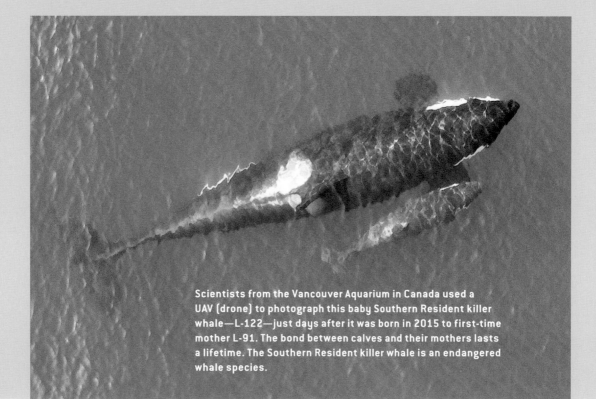

Scientists from the Vancouver Aquarium in Canada used a UAV (drone) to photograph this baby Southern Resident killer whale—L-122—just days after it was born in 2015 to first-time mother L-91. The bond between calves and their mothers lasts a lifetime. The Southern Resident killer whale is an endangered whale species.

In one set of photos, taken a year apart, the drone revealed two views of a family of orcas called L-pod. In the first shot, the mother swims with a newborn mottled gray calf and her older calf. The following year, the mother and her two calves—both a more mature black and white—swim together. "Future monitoring is going to tell us whether these calves survive and grow and recruit [become part of] the adult population," says Durban.

Q: What happens to baby whales when their mothers dive?

A: Whale mothers use babysitters! They leave their babies with other adult females or with juvenile (younger) whales while they dive.

GETTING SNOTTY

A drone called the SnotBot uses whale mucus to assess whale health. The Ocean Alliance, in Gloucester, Massachusetts, worked with nearby Olin College of Engineering to develop this research method. The person operating the drone wears a headset that shows what the drone "sees." The drone flies above a whale's highest spout (12 to 15 feet, or 3.7 to 4.6 m, for a sperm whale, and 30 feet, or 9.1 m, for a blue whale). SnotBot captures samples, including mucus, from the many exhalations a whale makes as it spouts. The SnotBot gathers mucus into collection tubes suspended over the whale's blow. "Believe it or not, exhaled breath condensate—or snot—is . . . priceless," Ocean Alliance leader Iain Kerr told Alyona Minkovski of the *Huffington Post*. "[From the snot], we're collecting viruses, bacteria, stress hormones, pregnancy hormones, and we're doing it without the cost of a major expedition." Scientists study the data from the samples in the lab to learn more about whale health.

In the past, researchers relied on biopsies—tissue samples cut from whale flesh—to study whale biology. SnotBots allow scientists to get the same information without the cut—and without disturbing the whale. Kerr got the idea for the SnotBot when he held up his two-year-old daughter to see a surfacing gray whale, and it blew mucus all over her. The experience planted a seed in Kerr's imagination. What if whale snot could be gathered another way?

The SnotBot team practices with a potato gun known as the SnotShot. It can blow at different heights and formations to represent the spouts of different whale species. The SnotShot is attached to a small boat (nicknamed the SnotYacht) that shoots fake snot into the air for the drone to capture. Eventually the Ocean Alliance hopes to send SnotBots to different whale habitats to assess different species and populations of whales. They hope to go first to the coast of Argentina to film southern right whales. Then they will film sperm whales in the Sea of Cortez to share data with scientists at the Autonomous University of Baja California Sur, La Paz in Mexico. Then on to Alaska and other whale habitats in other parts of the world.

FECES FINDINGS

Whale snot is not the only useful sample. Fecal (poop) samples help scientists understand how whales evolved from land to marine animals. Whale family trees share roots with giraffes and bison, land-based grazers that eat plants. Yet whales are carnivores. They eat the meat of shrimp, krill, and other sea animals. So the clues to their evolution lie in their guts, or digestive systems.

Ruminants—plant eaters, such as cows, that chew cud—have special guts lined with microbes (bacteria) that break down cellulose in the plants they eat. Peter Girguis, of Harvard University, and a team of specialists studied whale feces they found floating in the open sea. They compared it with samples from captive whales, including belugas at the Mystic Aquarium in Connecticut. The goal: to learn how whales use microbes to process their food.

Because whales eat meat, scientists expected them to share similar gut microbes—the bacteria that help process their food—with land carnivores such as tigers and wolves. And they do. The study also linked whale gut microbes to ruminant gut microbes. "The whale's foregut [a stomach with multiple chambers] is much like a cow's gut," Girguis said. Like cows, whales have gut microbes that break down a carbohydrate substance called chitin that forms the shells of shrimp and krill. The microbes do not break down the cellulose found in plants.

POOP-SNIFFING DOGS

Tucker, a black lab, works on a research boat in the Salish Sea, off the coast of Vancouver Island. Tucker's job is to get the poop on what's going on with whales in this area. He does it by using his nose to find fecal pellets—whale poop—in the water. Using a dog to sniff out whales was the idea of Roz Rolland at the New England Aquarium in Boston.

Off the coast of New England, right whale researchers relied on their own sight to spot floating rafts of orange whale poop in the ocean. But depending on eyesight was not efficient. So Rolland approached Samuel Wasser, the founder of Conservation Canines (CK9), a University of Washington program for training dogs to find scat (poop) in forests and fields. She asked Wasser to teach her to train dogs to find whale scat. Dogs are so good at this that more researchers, trainers, and dogs such as Tucker are getting into the act.

Tucker has a nose that can smell whale poop from far away. The dog also has a talent for communicating with his trainer without too much barking (which could scare the whales). When Tucker alerts to the poop, his trainer scoops up the sample and gives the dog a ball as a reward. And scientists get a window into the whale's life—a win-win situation all round.

Elizabeth Seely is a dog trainer for Seattle-based Conservation Canines. She holds Tucker as he sniffs for whale scat (feces) near San Juan Island, Washington. Tucker is the only working dog that is able to find and track the scent of orca scat in open water. Doing so helps marine biologists monitor the health of these endangered whales.

Studying the whale biome—the community of microbes in the whale's gut—helps explain more about the whale's family tree. It helps scientists get a little bit closer to understanding whales' connection to life on land. What's more, it shows how biomes change in related animals as their environment changes.

CHAPTER EIGHT
CAPTIVE WHALES

Orcas perform at SeaWorld Orlando. Since 2010, when a captive killer whale pulled veteran trainer Dawn Brancheau to her death there, SeaWorld and other aquariums have shifted their focus away from performance shows for the public and toward conservation efforts.

Most of our public has very little awareness of
wildlife and our impact on it. A close encounter
with a wild animal can really inspire them to make
a difference. The goal is to protect the
world's natural resources so there's no more
danger for animals. Until we get to that
point there's a crying need for the aquarium's
research and education efforts.

—Ken Ramirez, vice president of animal collections and training,
Shedd Aquarium, Chicago, 2011

A trip to brand-spanking-new Walt Disney World near Orlando, Florida, in
1975 often included a visit to SeaWorld Orlando. Visitors there delighted
in the resident orca that performed several times daily, willingly (or so it
seemed) grinning to show its row of white teeth, leaping out of its small pool for
fish rewards, belly flopping to splash the crowd. What a beautiful animal, kids
thought as they moved on to the dolphin show in a nearby tank. They envied
the trainers, including scientists studying orca learning and language. For many
kids, this was also a moment when they checked their conscience and realized
they weren't that comfortable with a whale of this size in a small, chlorinated
pool. Was it wrong? As people learned more about the lives of whales in the wild,
they questioned captivity more and more.

Keepers and trainers saw themselves as conservationists, not only by
looking after these individual whales but by allowing them to represent their
species. Whales in captivity could awe the public, many of whom had never seen
such a creature this close up or, most likely, at all. Audiences would be inspired,
the thinking went, to do more to preserve the whale habitat in the wild.

Cetaceans in captivity still provide a unique opportunity for researchers who
want to learn what makes whales tick and to use that understanding to study
the animals in the wild. For example, Chicago's Shedd Aquarium is among the few

WHALE TO WATCH: MAKOA

Makoa, a Pacific white-sided dolphin, was born June 1, 2015, in Chicago's Shedd Aquarium. The Shedd Aquarium is one of only four accredited institutions in the United States that is allowed to keep dolphins. The four institutions have twenty wild dolphins altogether.

Makoa is the second dolphin born at the Shedd. Makoa's mother is Piquet, aged twenty-seven. Makoa is her second calf. Her first, Sagu, was born in 2012. Shedd had had a difficult time getting started with its dolphin breeding program. (The aquarium has had dolphins since 1991.) Prior to Sagu's birth, four baby dolphins had died at the Shedd. Two were stillborn (born dead), and two died within days of birth. Aquarists clarify that these deaths are not uncommon in the wild, especially among first-time mothers.

The father of Piquet's babies is Lii, who lives at the Miami Seaquarium in Florida. To mate with Lii, staff transported Piquet to the Seaquarium, and a trainer confirmed that she was pregnant several months later.

aquariums authorized to care for breeding pairs and pregnant beluga whales. Its aquarists (caretakers for animals living in aquariums) work with colleagues in just four other aquariums nationwide to manage a small pod of captive beluga. Facilities like the Shedd Aquarium also take in and care for sick, injured, or orphaned cetaceans that sometimes cannot be released back into the wild.

CIRCUS CETACEANS

Some experts say that Henry Butler was the first to place a beluga in captivity when he found one stranded on a Massachusetts beach (far from its usual habitat) in 1861 and brought it to the Boston Aquarial and Zoological Gardens. There, staff kept it in a tank fed with water from Boston Harbor and trained the whale to pull a small boat shaped like a nautilus shell. The whale died after eighteen months from the stresses of life in captivity. During the whale's life at the Aquarial Gardens, one visitor was Sarah Gooll Putnam, an eleven-year-old who kept a diary. She sketched the whale and wrote, "I went again to the Aquarial Gardens and there we saw the Whale being driven by a girl. She was in a boat and the Whale was fastened to the boat by a pair of [reins] and a collar, which

Q:

What kinds of tricks can belugas learn?

A:

Belugas in captivity primarily learn tricks such as opening their mouths or sticking out their tongues or wagging their tails—behaviors they would not exhibit in the wild. They also learn to do natural behaviors on command, such as bubble blowing to find prey. Some belugas pick up other things, learning to mimic human voices and following children around as they walk in front of the glass of the enclosures.

was fastened round his neck. The men had to chase him before they could put on the collar." In the twenty-first century, a Boston eleven-year-old can ride a whale watch boat out of Boston Harbor to nearby Stellwagen Bank National Marine Sanctuary to see whales in the wild. But the 1860s were the height of commercial whaling, and few people observed live whales. Understanding their needs either in captivity or in the wild was a long way in the future.

In 1861 Phineas T. Barnum, the famous American circus owner, brought a pair of belugas from the seas of Labrador off the coast of eastern Canada to his American Museum in New York City. He transported the whales in boxes lined with seaweed and displayed them in a tank just 7 feet (2.1 m) deep. Thousands of visitors viewed the belugas before they died, after just two days. That didn't deter Barnum. Between 1861 and 1868, he sent a dozen more belugas to tanks in New York and Boston for display.

Since 1964, when the first orca was put on public display, Americans have been fascinated by this beautiful, intelligent animal. Whale and dolphin shows made people feel good. They learned about wildlife and knew that part of the ticket price went to research and care for whales. In the early 1990s, a nationwide poll found that 92 percent of Americans approved of ocean parks and felt they made an important contribution to education and the environment.

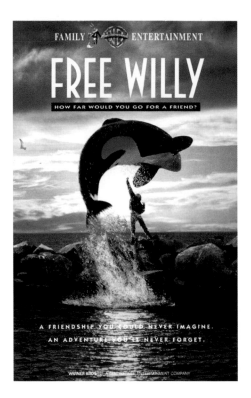

Popular films such as *Free Willy* (1993) have had a profound impact on the public attitude toward whales. These movies, along with documentary films about whales, have put pressure on aquariums and governments to stop breeding-in-captivity programs and to forbid the importation and exportation of wild cetaceans.

Most people were unaware of the price whales paid. Fishers, however, recalled feeling sad and guilty about taking little whales from their mothers to be raised in captivity. They were shocked when they saw the anguish of mother whales in response to losing their babies.

Public opinion altered further in 1993, when the movie *Free Willy* came out. This movie told the story of a captive whale and a boy's efforts to free him. The movie challenged the thinking of a generation of kids (and their parents). It focused their attention on the movie's star, a real orca called Keiko, that lived in a small pen in Mexico. In response to public demand after the film's release, Warner Brothers Studios led a fund-raiser to support rehabilitation to the wild for Keiko. Millions of schoolchildren donated. As a result, Keiko was moved first to a state-of-the-art rehabilitation facility in the sea off the coast of Oregon. Then Keiko went to a pen in his native waters, near Iceland. He was finally released into the open ocean and the company of other orcas. He died in 2003 in the ocean near Norway.

TROUBLE AT SEAWORLD

Animal welfare groups had protested captivity for many years. In 2010 a captive orca killed SeaWorld trainer Dawn Brancheau. The media and the American public joined the discussion. In 2013 the documentary *Blackfish* came out. Filmmaker Gabriela Cowperthwaite told the story of Tilikum, a male orca that had killed three people at SeaWorld Orlando. The film was difficult to watch. Viewers heard an interview with the diver who took Tilikum and three other calves from their mothers in the 1970s. They also learned about the stress that whales in captivity experience. The public's image of SeaWorld suffered greatly. Audiences diminished, and the park's stock prices took a dive. Americans were realizing just how much life in captivity differs from life in the wild. Tilikum, who was captured off the coast of Iceland in 1992, died in early 2017 at the age of thirty-six.

SeaWorld fought back, calling the documentary scientifically inaccurate and misleading. Yet research is showing that orcas are three times more likely to die at any age in captivity as they are in the wild. In part, this is due to the small tanks in which captive orcas live in aquariums. Even the largest orca tank provides only one-millionth of the range of the smallest range of an orca in the wild. In such a small space, orcas cannot get enough exercise and become dangerously out of shape. They are also negatively impacted emotionally by being in such tight quarters. In October 2015, in response to public pressure, the California Coastal Commission banned the breeding of killer whales in captivity. In March 2016, SeaWorld announced an end to the breeding program in all its parks. State lawmakers began to pass laws to prohibit capturing, importing, and exporting wild orcas. Over the next three years, SeaWorld committed to phasing out orca shows completely.

RETIREMENT AND REFUGE

In 2015 scientist Naomi Rose of the Animal Welfare Institute in Washington, DC, proposed the Whale Sanctuary Project. The idea was to create safe areas, such as sea pens or coves in coastal areas, to protect dolphins and whales. The areas would have netting to protect the animals from the dangers of the open sea. "They would offer the animals [a break] from performing and the constant exposure to a parade of strangers (an entirely unnatural situation for a species whose social groupings are based on family ties and stability. 'Strangers' essentially do not exist in orca society)," said Rose, who leads the organization. In May 2016, the organization announced plans to establish its first sanctuary for whales, dolphins, and porpoises.

SANCTUARY!

As early as 1914, Western Australian officials put an end to Norwegian whaling in a small area of the Indian Ocean. In 1938 the International Whaling Commission established the world's first whaling sanctuary—the Sanctuary. Located in Antarctica, the Sanctuary's goal was to protect one-quarter of Antarctica's whales from commercial whaling. Under pressure from whalers, the Sanctuary opened to commercial whaling in 1955. The whales could again be hunted legally, and the area's remaining baleen whales were practically wiped out. In response, the IWC established the 1982 moratorium on commercial whaling and reopened the area as the Southern Ocean Whale Sanctuary in 1994.

About fifteen years earlier, in 1979, the island nation known as the Republic of Seychelles joined the IWC to establish a second sanctuary, the Indian Ocean Whale Sanctuary. This sanctuary protects whales in their breeding and calving grounds.

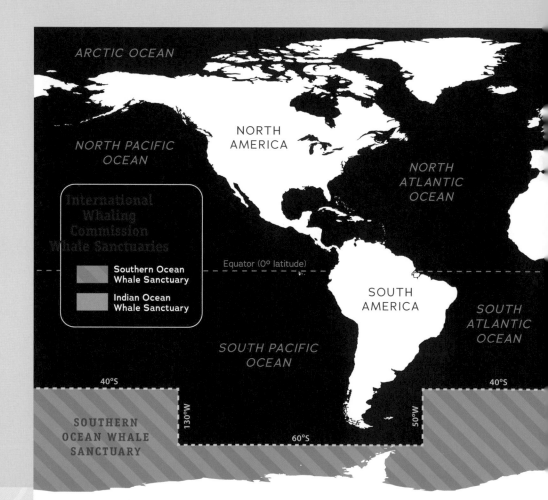

The Sanctuary extends from Africa to Australia and southward to the Southern Ocean Whale Sanctuary—the summer feeding grounds for up to 90 percent of the world's whales.

Japan still whales, claiming the nation is doing so under an agreement that allows nations to whale for scientific purposes. Japan believes it can legally whale within the sanctuaries' limits and has proposed lifting the ban on commercial whaling there but without success. Proposals for additional sanctuaries require the approval of three-quarters of IWC member nations. These proposals, as yet not approved, would create a third sanctuary in the international waters of the South Atlantic and South Pacific Oceans. Smaller sanctuaries, including the Australian Whaling Sanctuary and the Hawaiian Islands Humpback National Marine Sanctuary, protect whales within the boundaries of those regions.

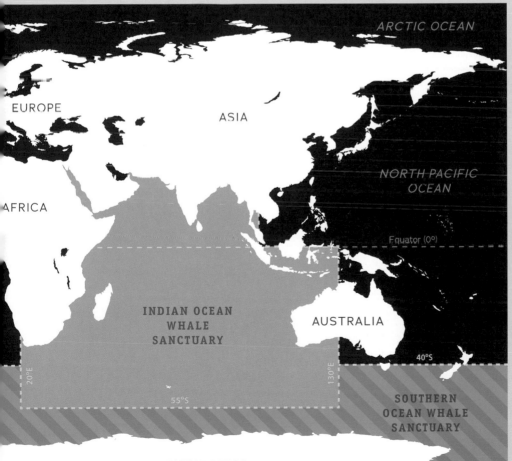

CHAPTER NINE
RESCUING WHALES

The US Coast Guard vessel *Kingfisher* helps members of the NOAA Fisheries and Florida Fish and Wildlife Conservation Commission free an entangled northern right whale off the coast of Jacksonville. A telemetry device and buoys help the team keep track of the whale.

> It was just insane. It was a
> very long four days.

—Peggy Stap, executive director and founder
of Marine Life Studies, describing the 2015 rescue
of an entangled humpback whale

For four days, a juvenile humpback whale led Peggy Stap and her team of researchers from the Whale Entanglement Team at Moss Landing, California, on a backbreaking trek up and down the coast of Monterey Bay. First spotted by whale watchers on a cruise, the whale was wrapped tightly in line from a crab pot that was later traced to Oregon, hundreds of miles to the north. A line ran across the whale's mouth and across its back. One flipper was caught in line that dug so deeply into the flesh that the team feared circulation would be cut off and infection would set in, resulting in the loss of the flipper.

After receiving news of the whale, Stap's rescue team boated out to carefully attach a telemetry buoy to the entangling lines. The buoy has a transmitter that sends a signal by satellite so the team can keep track of the whale's location. The entanglement team tracked this whale south, then north. Four days later, the team was finally able to cut the whale free of the line. The goal of rescuing whales from life-threatening conditions has led to innovations in technology and teamwork.

WHALE IN A WEB

Stormy Mayo was the first person licensed by the US government to rescue entangled whales. Mayo is responsible for developing many of the procedures associated with freeing whales. Like other rescue teams, the team at the CCS, where Mayo is a researcher, uses a rigid inflatable boat to approach an entangled whale. The team then puts a radio transmitter onto the whale to keep track of its whereabouts. The team also attaches sea anchors to slow down the animal. Rescuers never get into the water

A WHALE-SPOTTING DOG

Peggy Stap's dog Whiskie—a rescue mutt from an inland town in Michigan, has an unusual talent for spotting cetaceans. Whiskie goes to work with Stap, a scientist at Marine Life Studies in Moss Landing, on a research vessel in Monterey Bay. At first, Whiskie was just along for the ride. "I think she picked up on our excitement when we found whales and dolphins, so she started spotting them for us. All of a sudden, she'll run to the front or the back of the boat. I'll say, 'Something's around here!' and 95 percent of the time there's a whale or dolphin there." Stap thinks Whiskie responds to the high-pitched sound of certain dolphin calls. But Whiskie also gave her owner the heads-up about a blue whale on a day when there wasn't a ripple on the water.

with a whale because of the potential danger to both people and whales. Sometimes Mayo wears an ice hockey helmet with a video camera mounted on top to record his doings. Scott Landry, a whale researcher and artist, is often among the crew on the boat's first visit to an entangled whale. He helps assess the whale's situation and then creates a drawing to show exactly how the whale is entangled.

"It's very difficult to disentangle a whale on the first try," Landry says. So his first task—even before making the drawing—is to attach a telemetry buoy to the whale's back. The ability to track a whale increases the chances of the removal of all or at least some of the most dangerous parts of the whale's entanglement. These include lines that can cut off circulation or cause infection. The buoys—first used in 1999—can be a worry because they can add drag to an animal that may already be dragging. And the buoys can snag more fishing gear. Nonetheless, 80 percent of entangled whales tagged with buoys live. Only about 37 percent of whales that aren't tagged survive.

CUTTING ENTANGLEMENTS

Entanglements are most common in fishing areas and near a large population of people. They are also common in convergence zones, where ocean currents meet and debris drifts. For example, humpbacks migrating between Alaska and Hawaii to the south cross the Subtropical Convergence Zone twice a year—a recipe for trouble.

Sometimes an entangled whale has swum so far from the source of the line or debris that it's impossible to figure out where the trouble started. It can be difficult to know through which waters the whale has come.

Entangled whales meet several fates. They may die from wounds that lead to infection or from weights that make it impossible to come up for air and lead to drowning. They may drag heavy pots for so long they become exhausted and can no longer hunt for food. Some whales eventually get loose on their own and have the telltale scars and disfigurements to prove it. Other whales are able to go about their business even while entangled. Still others are freed by human rescue.

Red de Asistencia a Ballenas Enmalladas (RABEN), the Mexican Whale Disentanglement Network, is a successful rescue project that was launched in 2004. In 2006 David Mattila of the IWC began training RABEN rescue teams. Six years later, experienced rescuers—including Michael Moore of Woods Hole, Scott Landry of the Center for Coastal Studies, and Frances Gulland of the Marine Mammal Center in Sausalito, California—joined in.

RABEN has grown to fifteen teams with 180 trained members. They work in cooperation with the IWC and the Center for Coastal Studies to locate entangled whales. They try to remove lines and other debris to release the whales. Since 2004 they have successfully disentangled twenty-five whales. The majority (87 percent) of entangled whales in the bays along the Pacific coast of Mexico are humpbacks. More than half have been snagged in gill nets, and another 25 percent were trapped in lines. The group has begun working with local fishers to share information. The group is also educating them so they can help create a safer environment for whales.

Q:

What do whales drink?

A:

Whales never drink. They get their fluids from food, such as sand lance, a type of fish that is full of fresh water.

Ship Strikes

For a gigantic Panamax container ship on the ocean, hitting a whale can feel like a mere bump in the dark. The ships are so huge and powerful that they may actually show up in harbor with a whale's carcass on their bulging bow, unaware it is there until the ship makes port. Whales killed by ships may sink into the depths, float on the surface injured or dead, or wash up on beaches.

North Atlantic right whales swim parallel to the Atlantic coast of the United States and Canada. Their paths directly cross shipping routes into harbors. To avoid collisions with these whales, caring human captains have voluntarily responded by cutting speed and instituting aerial alert systems. Pilots in small planes spot whales and warn ships about their presence.

Moira "Mo" Brown of the New England Aquarium worked with Stormy Mayo on a model case. In 2003 she convinced the government of Canada to move shipping lanes in the Bay of Fundy to reduce ship collisions with right whales in this arm of the Atlantic Ocean. This was the first time in history that shipping lanes were adjusted to help an endangered marine species. And yet, not all shipping routes can be altered to avoid whales completely. For example, ships and sperm whales alike share the Straits of Gibraltar between Spain and North Africa. The best hope of avoiding collisions in this narrow, busy waterway is notification—and slower ships.

New technologies—including apps and social media—also aid in reducing danger for whales. Launched in 2012, Whale Alert is a NOAA app that meshes sightings of whales—live, dead, or distressed—with nautical "geosmart maps." The app notifies mariners and the public about the location of whale safety zones, which are regulated by the IWC. Between 2012 and the end of 2015, more than thirty thousand people—including citizen scientists and employees of research institutions and government agencies—had downloaded the app. Whale Alert raises awareness of whales in any area and reduces collisions.

Traffic Jam

Whale experts are well aware of the danger of ship strikes. They are less sure about whales' reactions to having a ship nearby. Tagging has helped researchers see that whales dive faster and come up slower when a ship is near. Their breathing also increases after an encounter with a ship. The breathing is evidence that as whales take evasive action, their stress level rises. Juvenile and injured whales are the most vulnerable to being hit by a boat. They are less experienced and less aware. They also spend more time at the surface, where encounters with ships are more likely.

John Calambokidis of the Cascadia Research Collective found that right whales and blue whales—among the scarcest of baleen whales—seem particularly sensitive to ship presence. Since their migration paths off the coast of California take them right through the Santa Barbara Channel, a major shipping lane, their stress levels are higher than whales of the same species that travel in less traffic.

MYSTERY ON THE BEACH

Whales near coasts may face another hazard: sonar. Over a period of several weeks in the winter of 2016, two dozen male sperm whales beached along the coast of the North Sea. They were found on coastal stretches in the United Kingdom, the Netherlands, and Germany. Experts couldn't say exactly why the whales had beached. They thought the whales may have followed a shoal (large number) of squid into the sea. Because the seafloor in the North Sea is not deep enough for whales, they became disoriented. Sperm whales use sonar in their deep-sea travels, but their sonar doesn't work in shallow sands.

At about that time, swimmers at a beach in Tiruchendur, India, came upon a pod of one hundred short-finned pilot whales. The glossy, blue-black whales flipped and flopped in the shallow waters. Rescuers rolled the whales back into the sea, and nearly half swam away—but without their leader. Others, too weak to swim out, washed back in again and died on the beach. Whale researcher Kumaran Sathasivam of the Marine Mammal Conservation Network of India told the BBC that stranded whales must be guided into deep water together. Otherwise, they will turn to stay near whales that are in distress. "The [stranded] whales [make] a sound that is not audible to human beings and that makes them return to the shore," Sathasivam said.

Five sperm whales, including this one, died on the Dutch North Sea island of Texel in January 2016. Experts aren't sure why the whales beached. When a whale is stranded onshore, it typically suffocates. If you run across a beached whale, immediately report it. Do not try to save it. This website lists contact information by state: http://www.nmfs.noaa.gov/pr/health/report.htm.

Whales are extremely social, so a whole pod may die because some of the whales are in trouble. In this case, the pod was left without a leader. More than forty-five of them swam back to shore and died on the beach.

Beached whales tend to suffocate because their bodies are not made to support their weight without water to buoy them. They dehydrate and their internal organs fail. If a person spots a beached whale in time and takes action by calling in experts, rescuers can keep the whale wet and push or tow the animal back out to sea.

Whales beach for various reasons. Orcas sometimes leap onto shore as they hunt seals. Sometimes a predator shark attacks a whale and the whale can no longer swim. Illness or wounds from ship strikes or fishing lines can also leave a whale too weak to swim. In these cases, the animal drifts to shore, where it may die. If the ailing drifter is one of the pod's leaders, the whole group may follow it to shore. Even healthy pilot whale leaders may chase prey into the shallows and unwittingly strand the whole pod.

How to Help a Stranded Marine Mammal

On February 14, 2011, Great Whale Conservancy scientists Gershon Cohen and Michael Fishbach and their families came upon a whale while boating in the Sea of Cortez. She was badly entangled in fishing gear, was struggling to breathe, and seemed near death. The group spent hours working to cut the tough plastic gill net that was wrapped tightly around her body.

The whale, which they named Valentina, returned to the rescue team a few minutes after being freed. They felt sure they understood what she was saying. She put on a show of breaching—about forty leaps in an hour—that could hardly be interpreted as anything but relief, joy, and perhaps even gratitude. To see the video of Valentina's rescue, visit this site: https://www.youtube.com/watch?v=tcXU7G6zhjU.

Rescue experts with NOAA's Fisheries' Marine Mammal Stranding Network advisory group recommend taking these actions if you spot a stranded whale or other marine animal:

- Don't push the animal back out to sea. It may be sick or injured.
- Immediately report your sighting of the stranded marine mammal or mammals, whether dead or alive, to the local marine mammal stranding network member. The website http://www.nmfs.noaa.gov/pr/health/report.htm lists contact information by state.
- When you make your report, e-mail or text a photo and GPS coordinates of the stranded animal to the network.
- Keep a safe distance from the animal. Stay with it until responders arrive so you can lead them to it.
- Minimize contact with the animal, and keep crowds away. Marine mammals may bite and can carry disease.

Clipper, a right whale, swims with her calf. Researchers can identify her by the notch in her flukes. She is catalogued as right whale #3450.

- Don't collect any parts (tissues, teeth, bones, or anything else) from dead animals. It is illegal and violates the Marine Mammal Protection Act.
- Don't attempt to remove any entangling line or gear.

Other agencies you can contact include these:

- the US Coast Guard over VHF radio on Channel 16
- the NOAA Fisheries Greater Atlantic Marine Animal Reporting Hotline at (866) 755-NOAA (6622) for the Atlantic coast or (877) SOS-WHALE, which partners with NOAA to cover the coasts of Washington and Oregon coasts
- NOAA Fisheries Stranding Hotline at (877) 925-7773 for stranded Cook Inlet beluga whales

WHALE TO WATCH: CLIPPER AND HER CALF

The mother right whale and her calf *(facing page)* surfaced in Sebastian Inlet, an entrance to the Indian River lagoon along the Atlantic coast of Florida. Had the calf tired of swimming at sea and drifted in? Had the mother led or followed? Were they stuck in the inlet because of the current of the rising tide? No one could say for sure.

Spectators swarmed the bridge that crossed the inlet and lined the shores of the nearby state park, thrilling at the sight of these rare and unusual whales. Florida Fish and Wildlife Conservation Commission officials shut down the harbor to boat traffic. Staff members from Hubbs-SeaWorld Research Institute counted the whales' breaths, figured they were acting normally—and in no distress. They identified the mother whale by the telltale notch in her tail flukes. She was Clipper, right whale #3450, from the North Atlantic Right Whale catalogue. And her 20-foot (6.1 m) calf? Too new to name.

Allison Lees Heater, a deep-sea researcher who happened to be ashore, went to watch. As the tide went slack, the whales made several passes toward the bridge (which crosses the inlet). Each time the mother reached the bridge's shadow, she would turn around, seeming frightened. Heater suggested, "Maybe passing too closely to a large shadowy object led to her tail injury (which was old and well healed over)." On her sixteenth try, Clipper went under the bridge at last, and the calf went with her. For a day or two, conservation commission officials tracked the pair with airplane flyovers. All signs indicated that the pair had gotten through their detour in good shape.

CHAPTER TEN

CITIZEN WHALE SCIENCE

Blue whales are the largest animal known to have existed on Earth. The adults can weigh as much as 220 tons (200 metric tons). Belonging to the rorqual family, blues have longitudinal pleats that allow the throat to expand. This helps the whales swallow huge gulps of water, straining out krill and other small fish or plankton through their baleen. An adult blue can eat 6 tons (5.4 metric tons) or more of food every day.

Whales, we now know, teach and learn.
They scheme. They cooperate, and they grieve.
They recognize themselves and their friends.
They know and fight back against their enemies.
And perhaps most stunningly,
given all of our transgressions against them,
they may even, in certain circumstances,
have learned to trust us again.

—Charles Siebert, "Watching Whales Watching Us," *New York Times Magazine*, July 8, 2009

Science is changing! Researchers who once kept data to themselves are now sharing it, a trend that focuses energy on asking new questions—and combining everybody's data to tease out the answer. Increasingly, experts reach outside the scientific world to tap a vital resource: whale watchers, who can lend fresh eyes, ears, and insights. New technology is making citizen scientists of the whales themselves.

In the past, knowledge of whales came to laypeople (nonscientists) through cultural and family traditions or through educational experiences. Whale watching was limited to those who could see whales from shore. Since whale watching from boats that travel out to sea has become more popular, so too has whale watchers' involvement in whale research. Whale watches feed a growing sense of human responsibility toward the ocean environment and a sense of being united with the natural world. Through modern communications—computers and smartphones—people can tell one another about whales and connect with scientists, offering up-to-the-minute data.

In 2000 whale watchers in Monterey Bay, California, spotted something never seen there before—orcas from the K- and L-pods. These pods usually live off the coasts of British Columbia and Washington, 1,000 miles (1,609 km) away. "Scientists can only be so many places at once," says naturalist Sarah

INSIDER TIPS

Volunteer programs at aquariums and other research/exhibition centers provide ways for teenagers to get valuable experience with ocean science. Donna Hauser is a scientist at the Polar Science Center at the University of Washington. She is researching the impact of climate change on whale food sources. She offers these additional insights and advice on becoming a whale scientist:

1. **Specialize.** "You can't say you want to study just anything about marine mammals. You can't be a jack-of-all-trades [generalist]. Zero in on something, whether it's acoustics, movements and position, health effects (you could take the vet approach), genetics, or climate change. There are lots of different lines of inquiry."

2. **Be adventurous.** "If you're interested in whales and dolphins, it can be hard to get taken seriously as a scientist. Go find a respected researcher that you're interested in working with!" Partnering with a mentor is a key part of becoming established in a field.

3. **Do the math.** "Have some really solid math and science and computer science [skills]. I spend much more time behind a computer than I do in the field. It's important to prove that you're an independent scientist at a young age."

Wilson Finstuen. "More eyes and cameras on whales is a huge bonus in helping scientists with population studies and behavioral observations."

Finstuen describes one way that social media is a powerful assistant to people learning about whales. "Sometimes the whale watching experience gives people more awareness and the ability to feel confident of what they're seeing. This year off Oceanside [California] we could see feeding orcas from the fishing pier. People on the pier who wondered what these whales were called into the local news. My Facebook was flooded. 'Yes, they're orcas!' we answered. And then through social media we were able to track this transient [traveling] female pod as they made their way up the coastline."

People post their pictures from whale watches on Flickr, Facebook, Instagram, Twitter, and other social media sites, letting one another know where whales are and exchanging images and information that can help with whale movement trends and identifications of individual whales. Some are even posting extra-cute images, such as a baby beluga whale that seems to be smiling for the camera. Viewers are drawn to these faces—and drawn into discussions of the challenges the animals face. Whale watch naturalists post blogs with photos of the whales they've seen each day and link to aquariums and research institutions so people can learn more. As they have since the 1970s, scientists work aboard whale watch boats to share information and make observations. They are starting to narrow down the data they want. They also want to figure out ways to make whale watchers and boaters part of their research teams through social media and smartphone apps.

ANYONE MAY APPLY

Lei Lani Stelle developed a smartphone app called Whale mAPP. It allows people on boats to map their trips and record sightings of marine mammals right into the maps. Courtney Hann, a graduate student at Oregon State University, joined forces with Alaska Whale Foundation director Andy Szabo to organize the citizen science Whale mAPP program. They recruit boaters, tourists, and naturalists to make the app part of their voyages. Anybody can sign up to use it, so the Whale mAPP community—and data—are expected to swell. Among the most faithful contributors are young people, teens, and elementary students. Whale mAPP data encompasses findings from southeastern Alaska, Washington, and Northern California—as well as spots in Russia, Greenland, and the Caribbean.

Whale mAPP users document weather conditions and details about the whales they spotted. This includes species, number of whales, their age, and whether calves are present. The data is uploaded to scientists who use it to add to their understanding of whale habitats and behaviors. Hann says, "The first step was to learn how reliable the Whale mAPP findings were: could everyday people (as opposed to scientists) identify whales and recognize trends, such as learning where whales feed or sea lions haul out?" The answer was yes, which was good news for science. "In a hundred sightings of humpback whales, even when you looked at areas less used by the whales, the quality of the sightings by experts and novices was the same." Another benefit? Hann found that Whale mAPP users became better at identifying and observing marine mammals as a result of the app.

WHALE WATCHERS: BIOLOGIST KRISTIN LAIDRE

Kristin Laidre, a principal scientist for the Polar Science Center, works in the Far North. She studies the narwhal, a small toothed whale with a long, twisted horn. Getting to narwhal territory is a quest as arduous as that of any unicorn-hunting knight. "The Arctic is a complicated place to work. You're dealing with chunks of sea ice or frozen ocean. All your equipment freezes, and it's very difficult," she says.

Narwhals live far offshore, so Laidre and her team set up a base (a little hut) on a strip of coast near where she knows the mammals will pass. She flies by helicopter to open waters at the edge of the sea ice. Then she climbs into a small inflatable

Often called the unicorn of the ocean, the narwhal is a unique and rare type of toothed whale. Its distinctive tusk is actually a tooth that grows only from the upper jaw of males.

boat to look for the whales. "By nature narwhals are shy, skittish animals. They're easily spooked, so doing any kind of study of them means you have to sneak up on them. You camouflage yourself in white, don't make a lot of noise, have a net in the water, and hope a whale . . . swims into the net." Laidre takes tissue samples from the whales she nets and then releases the animals back into the sea. She also studies the waters in which they live.

Laidre consults with indigenous peoples who rely on hunting whales for their food and as part of their culture. They sometimes share interesting observations. For example, one man found sixteen whole, fresh halibut in the stomach of a narwhal he had hunted. In turn, Laidre shares her information with the locals. "We share our maps and other information with the local people and with people making management decisions about the area."

Finding the World's Biggest Whale

Antarctic blue whales are critically endangered. In the twenty-first century, they are rarely seen and poorly understood. Where did they go? What do they eat? Scientists didn't have much information. Leigh Torres of Oregon State University had heard of sightings of blue whales during an industrial seismic survey in the South Taranaki Bight, a body of water between the northern and southern islands of New Zealand. These tests involve sound waves that can penetrate the subseafloor (beneath the sea bottom). Blues were unheard of—but also unstudied—in this bight. Torres looked to local reports going back to the nineteenth century to learn more. She pored over whaling logs of the 1950s to the 1970s from the Soviet Union (a union of fifteen republics including Russia, 1922–1991). Torres also found stories of sightings from local tugboat crews and other ships. With this information, she mapped more blue whale sightings and strandings in the bight. She wondered why the whales would be in the bight. The answer? A seasonal coastal upwelling—an upward flow of nutrient-rich water from the bottom of the water. The food source that attracts the blues is the euphausiids, a type of zooplankton.

In December 2015, Torres reported on her research to a group of twenty-five hundred scientists from eighty countries. They had met to compare their notes on the lives of marine mammals. She made a passionate plea to the group about space-use conflicts. She described that the bight is an area teaming with oil platforms, seabed mining, vessel traffic, and pipelines. Whales are likely to lose out in this habitat, overtaken by human industry. Torres cautions, "If we don't raise our voices and challenge industry, then who will communicate the facts and advocate for change?" Scientific information, she says, can help convince government leaders and the public to change policies, improve whale environments, and make a difference in the future of whales on Earth. In late 2016, Bruce Mate, director of the Marine Mammal Institute at Oregon State University, announced a new partnership—between humans and whales. With Advanced Dive Behavior (ADB) tags, sperm whales gather second-by-second data that gives detailed information about where whales dive and migrate and how they interact with prey. Mate told *Science Daily*, "We're learning more about whales, and whales are helping us to learn more about our own planet."

THE WHALES ARE MISSING!

Humpbacks belong to small pods of two to fifteen whales. They are favorites among whale watchers for the displays of breaching and slapping of pectoral fins and tails on the surface of the water. Experts and citizen scientists are working together to better understand whale behavior as part of a global effort to protect cetaceans.

We're just beginning to understand what the ocean looks like from a whale's point of view.

—Joe Roman, quoted in *Voyaging in the Wake of the Whale*
exhibit, Mystic Seaport, Connecticut, n.d.

In the news as this book went to press was a story from Hawaii. Every winter, humpbacks arrive at this southern point of their annual migration—a journey of thousands of miles. Ten thousand North Pacific humpbacks swim all the way from Alaska to mate and give birth in Hawaii's warm waters. Once they arrive, social media lights up like the signs in Times Square in New York City. In Hawaii everyone heads to shore. You don't even need a whale watch boat to see the whales!

Cars crowd cliffside overlooks. Beachgoers with binoculars train their lenses on the horizon. And plenty of people can spy the big slate-gray and snow-white whales with just their own two eyes. From shore, they watch for hours as the whales breach, lobtail (slap their tails on the surface), roll, flop and, in general, frisk around. Calves seem to be having the most fun. They splash and slap, imitating their parents. You've never seen a baby shower like this!

In winter 2016, the humpbacks were late. Each year volunteers for the Humpback Whale National Marine Sanctuary count the whales they see, clipboards in their laps. "We've [only] seen a handful of whales," said Ed Lyman, the response coordinator of the sanctuary, a shallow, 600-foot (183 m) area off the coast of the Hawaiian Islands of Kaua'i, Maui, Oahu, and Hawaii. The sanctuary is one of the world's most important habitats for humpbacks.

Lyman thinks that perhaps El Niño, a seasonal warm-water pattern, had shifted feeding spots for the whales that year. And far to the north, where the whales feed all summer, warming waters have attracted more whales. This means whales in Arctic waters have to compete harder for their food. And working harder for food means they have less energy for the long migration to Hawaii.

Breaching is one of the most spectacular and graceful whale behaviors that humans witness. Scientists are not exactly sure why whales breach.

But Lyman isn't worried. "It's an example of the variability of Mother Nature. One theory [is] that something like this happened as whales increased. It's a product of their success." As the media picked up on the mystery of the "missing" humpbacks, experts responded that the whales weren't missing at all, just later than usual. Whale watchers said the numbers were normal—the timing was just off. Maybe the migration was slowed by El Niño or changes in food or something else entirely. When it comes to whales, sometimes all you can do is shrug. To find out for sure, we'll need more research, more technology, more eyes and ears on the sea, more ideas—and imagination to consider possible story lines. The storytellers will be the next generation of whale watchers.

Q:

Do whales sleep?

A:

Whales have to keep half their brains awake as they sleep to keep up the voluntary breathing they have to do to stay alive. (Humans breathe automatically and involuntarily so our entire brain can go to sleep.)

WHALE GUIDE

This guide includes a sampling of some of the world's most watched whales. Whales are divided into two suborders: baleen and toothed whales. For more details about whale, dolphin, and porpoise species, check out the Further Information section.

BALEEN WHALES

Baleen whales (mysticetes) are a suborder that includes the world's largest whales, blue whales, and others with a comblike curtain of baleen in the mouth with which they filter food from the water.

BLUE WHALE

Scientific name	*Balaenoptera musculus* (big-winged mouse-whale)
Length	up to 110 feet (33 m)
Weight	up to 300,000 pounds (136,078 kg)
Diet	krill
Appearance	gray color that looks light blue when seen through the water
Status	estimated 5,000, down from an estimated pre-whaling population of 200,000

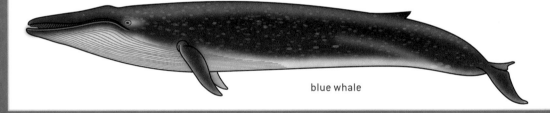

blue whale

BOWHEAD WHALE

Scientific name	*Balaena mysticetus* (mustached whale)
Length	35 to 40 feet (11 to 12 m)
Weight	150,000 to 200,000 pounds (68,039 to 90,718 kg)
Diet	zooplankton (krill and copepods), fish, and invertebrates
Appearance	dark body with a white chin (mustache), bow-shaped head, no dorsal fin
Status	estimated 100,000 (the Gulf of Mexico bowhead whale—endangered)

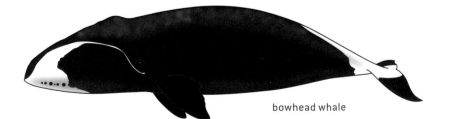

bowhead whale

FIN (OR FINBACK OR FINNER) WHALE

Scientific name	*Balaenoptera physalus* (whale that blows)
Length	75 to 85 feet (22 to 26 m)
Weight	80,000 to 160,000 pounds (36,287 to 72,575 kg)
Diet	krill and small schooling fish such as herring and sand lance
Appearance	chevrons (a modified V pattern) behind the blowhole; a sharp ridge, or razorback, from dorsal fin to tail fluke; a large, curving dorsal fin
Status	8,000, down from a 120,000 pre-whaling population

fin whale

GRAY WHALE

Scientific name	*Eschrichtius robustus* (devil fish)
Length	50 feet (15 m)
Weight	80,000 pounds (36,287 kg)
Diet	bottom-feeders—benthic (seafloor) amphipods
Appearance	gray body with a dorsal "hump" rather than a fin and bumps called "knuckles" along its back; distinctive tail flukes, with an S-shaped trailing edge and a deep middle notch
Status	19,000 to 23,000 eastern North Pacific gray whales (delisted—removed from the endangered species list—due to recovery to near their original number); status not known for western North Pacific (endangered); North Atlantic gray whales are extinct

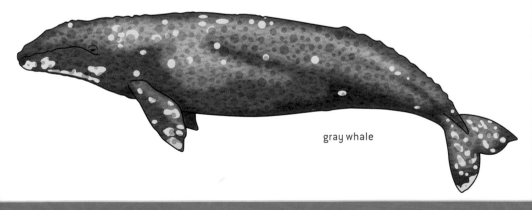

gray whale

HUMPBACK WHALE

Scientific name:	*Megaptera novaeangliae* (big-winged New Englander)
Length:	up to 60 feet (18 m)
Weight:	50,000 to 80,000 pounds (22,680 to 36,287 kg)
Diet:	small fish, sand lance, herring, and krill
Appearance:	dark gray with white accents on tail flukes; white flippers and underside; knobby tubercles, sometimes with one hair, on their heads
Status:	estimated 10,000

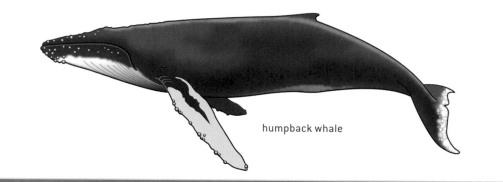

humpback whale

MINKE WHALE

Scientific name:	*Balaenoptera acutorostrata* (sharp-snouted winged whale)
Length:	up to 33 feet (10 m)
Weight:	up to 20,000 pounds (9,072 kg)
Diet:	small fish, herring, capelin, and krill
Appearance:	black flippers with a white band; some with a chevron on the back, behind the blowhole
Status:	estimated 500,000

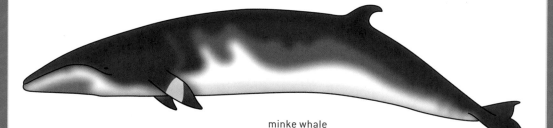

minke whale

OMURA'S WHALE

Scientific name:	*Balaenoptera omurai* (Omura's whale)
Length:	33 to 38 feet (10 to 12 m)
Weight:	unknown
Diet:	schooling fish
Appearance:	similar in coloration to fin whales, with an asymmetrical lower jaw that is white on the right and dark on the left; a prominent ridge on the rostrum (top of the head)
Status:	unknown

Omura's whale

RIGHT WHALES

Right whales are part of the *Eubalaena* genus (classification group) of large baleen whales.

NORTH ATLANTIC RIGHT WHALE

Scientific name:	*Eubalaena glacialis* (true whale)
Length:	50 feet (15 m)
Weight:	up to 140,000 pounds (63,503 kg)
Diet:	small organisms, krill, and copepods
Appearance:	no dorsal fin; heads may be marked distinctively with callosities, or light-colored crusty skin growths
Status:	600, with an estimated 500 of these in the western North Atlantic

North Atlantic right whale

NORTH PACIFIC RIGHT WHALE

Scientific name:	*Eubalaena japonica* (Japanese right whale)
Length:	45 to 55 feet (14 to 17 m)
Weight:	110,000 to 180,000 pounds (49,895 to 81,647 kg)
Diet:	zooplankton, including euphausiids, copepods, and cyprids
Appearance:	similar to the North Atlantic right whale
Status:	fewer than 500 whales, down from a pre-whaling estimate of 11,000

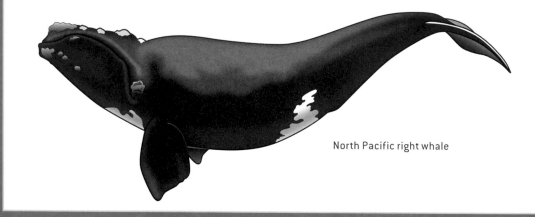

North Pacific right whale

SOUTHERN RIGHT WHALE

Scientific name:	*Eubalaena australis* (southern or Australian right whale)
Length:	46 to 49 feet (14 to 15 m)
Weight:	88,000 to 150,000 pounds (39,916 to 68,039 kg)
Diet:	zooplankton
Appearance:	similar to other right whales, with a large callosity at the front of the head called the bonnet
Status:	estimated at 7,000 in 2001, down from a pre-whaling estimate of 60,000

southern right whale

PYGMY RIGHT WHALE

Scientific name:	*Caperea* (wrinkle) *marginata* (dark border around the baleen)
Length:	20 feet (6.1 m)
Weight:	9,920 pounds (4,500 kg)
Diet:	copepods and krill
Appearance:	flippers darker than the rest of its body; curved dorsal flipper
Status:	unknown

pygmy right whale

SEI WHALE

Scientific name:	*Balaeaonoptera borealis* (northern winged whale)
Length:	up to 40 to 60 feet (12 to 18 m)
Weight:	up to 100,000 pounds (45,359 kg)
Diet:	plankton, fish, and squid
Appearance:	a slim, streamlined whale that is light underneath with dark shades of blue, purple, and gray above; sometimes confused with Bryde's whales
Status:	up to 80,000, down from a pre-whaling population of 300,000

sei whale

ODONTOCETES (TOOTHED WHALES)
BEAKED WHALES

Beaked whales are a classification group of toothed whales that includes Baird's and Cuvier's beaked whales. These whales have very long rostrums (beaks, or bills).

BAIRD'S BEAKED WHALE

Scientific name:	*Berardius bairdii* (*Berardius* comes from the last name of Auguste Bérard, a nineteenth-century French captain of a ship transporting a type of whale later named after him)
Length:	42 feet (13 m)
Weight:	20,000 pounds (9,072 kg)
Diet:	deep-dwelling fish, squid, and octopus
Appearance:	small head with a bulbous forehead; lower jaw extends 4 inches (10 centimeters) beyond its upper jaw, exposing its teeth; dark in color, with shadings from blue to brown or black, with a light gray underside
Status:	unknown

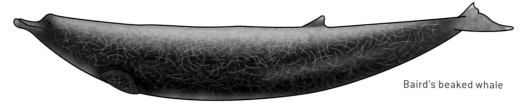

Baird's beaked whale

CUVIER'S BEAKED WHALE

Scientific name:	*Ziphius cavirostris* (goosebeak whale)
Length:	23 feet (7 m)
Weight:	5,500 pounds (2,495 kg)
Diet:	mostly squid and some fish or crabs
Appearance:	turned-up mouth that looks like a goose's; coloring changes throughout the whales' lives, ranging from rust to tan to gray, with old male whales often having white heads
Status:	unknown

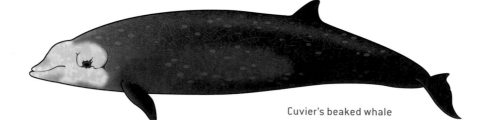

Cuvier's beaked whale

ORCA

Scientific name:	*Orcinus orca* (killer whale)
Length:	up to 30 feet (9 m)
Weight:	up to 18,000 pounds (8,165 kg)
Diet:	squid, big fish, whales, and seals
Appearance:	black backs with white undersides, with an oval white patch behind each eye; a gray "saddle" patch behind the dorsal fin, which varies among individual whales
Status:	unknown

orca

DOLPHINS AND PORPOISES

Dolphins are the largest family of cetaceans, with between thirty-two and thirty-seven species. Although there are more bottlenose than any other kind of dolphin, their numbers have been depleted in some areas, so they are a protected species. Dolphins are small odontocetes with round teeth. Porpoises are a small group of odontocetes with only seven species. They have spade-shaped teeth.

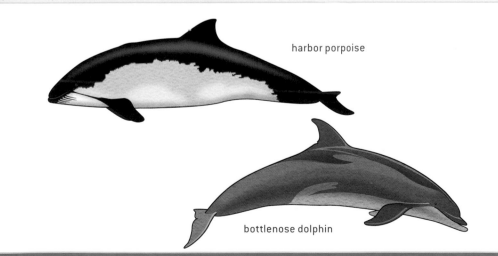

harbor porpoise

bottlenose dolphin

WHITE WHALES

BELUGA WHALE

Scientific name:	*Delphinapterus leucas* (canary of the sea or sea canary or melon head)
Length:	14 to 16 feet (4 to 5 m)
Weight:	3,000 to 3,500 pounds (1,361 to 1,588 kg)
Diet:	fish (especially salmon), crabs, shrimp, and sandworms
Appearance:	small head with a melon (bulbous forehead); no dorsal fin, which helps belugas swim below ice; and cervical vertebrae (the bones in the neck) not fused (immobilized), allowing head movement
Status:	up to 200,000

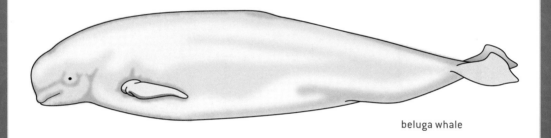

beluga whale

NARWHAL

Scientific name:	*Monodon monoceros* (single tooth, single horn)
Length:	13 to 15 feet (4 to 4.6 m)
Weight:	2,000 to 3,500 pounds (907 to 1,588 kg)
Diet:	cod, squid, and other fish in deep inlets and bays
Appearance:	a stocky gray-brown whale with a light underside; male's tusk with a reach of 9 feet (2.7 m); no dorsal fin
Status:	about 50,000

narwhal

PILOT WHALES (OR BLACKFISH)

Pilot whales are a group of toothed whales that include long- and short-finned whales.

LONG-FINNED AND SHORT-FINNED PILOT WHALE

Scientific name:	*Globicephala melas* (long-finned; name means "black sphere head")
	Globicephala macrorhynchus (short-finned; name means "sphere head, long snout")
Length:	up to 20 feet (6 m)
Weight:	2,200 to 6,000 pounds (998 to 2,722 kg)
Diet:	mostly squid, sometimes octopus, cuttlefish, herring, and other fish
Appearance:	long-finned pilot whales with long flippers one-eighth their body length, all with a grayish-white anchor-shaped patch on the underside with the base of the anchor on the throat; the short-finned is distinguished by a white saddle patch behind the dorsal fin
Status:	almost 1 million long-finned and about 200,000 short-finned

short-finned pilot whale

long-finned pilot whale

SPERM WHALE

Scientific name:	*Physeter macrocephalus* (the big-headed blower)
Length:	49 to 59 feet (15 to 18 m)
Weight:	32,000 pounds (14,515 kg)
Diet:	squid, tuna, barracuda, and sharks
Appearance:	purplish-gray or black whale with teeth only on the lower jaw; has a waxy whitish oil (which looks like human sperm) inside its big, square head
Status:	about 360,000, down from an estimated 1 million pre-whaling population

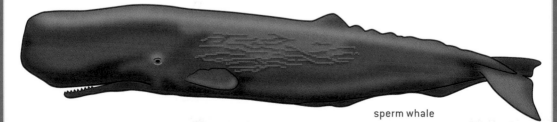

sperm whale

SOURCE NOTES

5 Philip Hoare, *The Whale: In Search of the Giants of the Sea* (New York, Ecco, 2010), 30.

9 Natalie Schmitt to Ann Jones, "Hear a Symphony of Whale Song," *Off Track, Australian Broadcasting Corporation*, November 9, 2015, http://www.abc.net.au/radionational/programs /offtrack/antarctic-blue-whale-song-worlds-biggest-choir/6919222.

16 The Holy Bible, Jonah 1:17–2:10 (King James Version) (New York: Collins' Clear-Type, 1957), 853.

17 MacGillivray Freeman's *Humpback Whales* final production notes, 2015, MacGillivray Freeman Films and Pacific Life, http://www.macgillivrayfreemanfilms.com/site/media/humpback_whales /assets/HW_Production_Notes.pdf.

19 Hoare, *Whale*, 122.

22 Randall R. Reeves and Tim D. Smith, Northeast Fisheries Science Center Reference Document 03-12, "A Taxonomy of World Whaling: Operations, Eras, and Sources," NOAA, September 15, 2003, http://nefsc.noaa.gov/publications/crd/crd0312/.

23 Salvatore Cerchio, quoted in "First Ever Confirmed Sightings of Omura's Whales in the Wild," New England Aquarium, October 26, 2015, http://news.neaq.org/2015/10/new-video-of-nearly -unknown-whale.html.

25 Nelson Cole Haley, *Journal, 1849–1853*, Mystic Seaport, 47–48, http://library.mysticseaport .org/initiative/PageImage.cfm?PageNum=47&BibID=30775, http://library.mysticseaport.org /initiative/PageImage.cfm?PageNum=48&BibID=30775.

29 Anne Witty, guest curator, quoted at *Voyaging in the Wake of the Whales*," Mystic Seaport, author visit, August 2015.

36 Roy Ahmaogak, Ilisagvik College, Barrow Alaska, interview with author, June 29, 2010.

39 James Higham, Lars Bejder, and Rob Williams, "Tourism, Cetaceans, and Sustainable Development: Moving beyond Simple Binaries and Intuitive Assumptions," *Whale-Watching: Sustainable Tourism and Ecological Management* (Cambridge: Cambridge University Press, 2014), 2.

40 Wayne Perryman, "Gray Whale Health Update," video, *Voices in the Sea* online exhibit, accessed August 24, 2016, http://cetus.ucsd.edu/voicesinthesea_org/videos/videoGrayUpdate.html.

40 Chad Avellar, interview with author, August 2015.

44 Peter T. Stevick, Mariana C. Neves, Freddy Johansen, Marcia H. Engel, Judith Allen, Milton C. C. Marcondes, and Carole Carlson, "A Quarter of a World Away: Female Humpback Whale Moves 10,000 Km between Breeding Areas," *Biology Letters* 7, no. 2 (April 23, 2011): 299–302, http://rsbl.royalsocietypublishing.org/content/7/2/299.

45 E. C. M. Parsons, "The Negative Impacts of Whale-Watching," *Journal of Marine Biology* 2012 (2012), http://www.hindawi.com/journals/jmb/2012/807294/.

47 Sarah Wilson Finstuen, phone interview with author, March 17, 2015.

50–51 Jooke Robbins, e-mails and phone interview with author, November 2015.

51 Ibid.

52 Michelle Fournet, "Listening to the Past," Alaska Whale Foundation, accessed August 23, 2016, http://www.alaskawhalefoundation.org/blog/2014/8/26/listening-to-the-past.

58 Roger Payne, "Humpback Whale Conservation," video, *Voices in the Sea* online exhibit, accessed August 24, 2016, http://cetus.ucsd.edu/voicesinthesea_org/videos/videoHumpback Cons.html.

59 Ibid.

59–60 Jim Darling, "Why Do They Sing?," video, *Voices in the Sea* online exhibit, accessed August 24, 2016, http://cetus.ucsd.edu/voicesinthesea_org/videos/videoHumpbackSong.html.

61 Mark Baumgartner, phone interview with author, November 24, 2015.

62 Christopher Willes Clark, quoted in Marissa Fessenden, "Maybe the World's Loneliest Whale Isn't So Isolated, after All," *Smithsonian*, April 15, 2015, http://www.smithsonianmag.com/smart -news/maybe-worlds-loneliest-whale-isnt-so-isolated-after-all-180955005/?no-ist.

64 Howard Hall, quoted in MacGillivray Freeman's *Humpback Whales* final production notes, 2015, http://www.macgillivrayfreemanfilms.com/site/media/humpback_whales/assets/ HW_Production_Notes.pdf.

66 Fournet, "Listening to the Past."

66 Ibid.

66 "Does Military Sonar Kill Wildlife?," *Scientific American*, June 10, 2009, http://www .scientificamerican.com/article/does-military-sonar-kill/.

67 Virginia Morell, "U.S. Navy to Limit Sonar to Protect Whales," *Science*, September 16, 2015, http://www.sciencemag.org/news/2015/09/us-navy-limit-sonar-testing-protect-whales.

69 Peter Tyack, "Future Directions in Marine Mammal Science," Plenary session, 21st Biennial Conference of the Biology of Marine Mammals, San Francisco, December 14, 2015.

70 Fred Sharpe, quoted in "Whale's Eye View," *National Geographic* Crittercam video, accessed August 24, 2016, http://video.nationalgeographic.com/video/crittercam/whale_humpback _crittercam.

72 John Durban, to Rich Press, "On the Line," podcast, NOAA, October 21, 2015, http://www.nmfs .noaa.gov/podcasts/2015/10/uav_killer_whale.html.

73 John Durban, quoted in Frances C. Robertson, W. R. Koski, T. A. Thomas, J. R. Brandon, W. J. Richardson, B. Würsig, and A. W. Trites, "A Question of Availability: Seismic Survey Sound Affects the Visual Detectability of Bowhead Whales," conference poster, Alaska Marine Science Symposium, Anchorage, Alaska, January 2013, http://www.distantfin.net/uploads/6/5/4/8 /6548806/fcr_amss_2013.jpg.

73 Iain Kerr, quoted in Jared Greenhouse, "Snot Bot Drone Aids Whale Research by Collecting You-Know-What," *Huffington Post*, July 24, 2015, http://www.huffingtonpost.com/entry/snotbot -drone-aids-in-whale-research_us_55b12a0ee4b08f57d5d3ef15.

74 Peter Girguis, e-mail conversation with author, October 5, 2015.

77   Ken Ramirez, Shedd Aquarium, phone interview with author, April 19, 2011.

78–79 Sarah Gooll Putnam, diaries, February 22–23, 1862, in the collection of the Massachusetts Historical Society, http://www.masshist.org/database/382.

81   Naomi A. Rose, "A Win-Win Solution for Captive Orcas and Marine Theme Parks," *CNN*, last modified October 28, 2013, http://www.cnn.com/2013/10/24/opinion/blackfish-captive -orcas-solutions/.

85   Peggy Stap, quoted in Caitlin Conrad, "Entangled Humpback Freed near Farrallon Islands after 4-Day Chase," *KSBW*, July 8, 2015, http://www.ksbw.com/news/entangled-humpback-freed -near-big-sur-after-4day-chase/34043902.

86   Peggy Stap, quoted in Joe Truskot and Jay Dunn, "Whiskie the Whale Spotter," video, *Californian*, December 1, 2014, http://www.thecalifornian.com/videos/life/2014/12/01/19736687/.

86   Scott Landry, "Principles, Guidelines and a Strategy for Building Capacity to Respond to Entangled Large Whales: Building a Global Whale Entanglement Response Network," speaking in a group presentation at 21st Biennial Conference on the Biology of Marine Mammals, San Francisco, December 17, 2015.

89   Kumaran Sathasivam, quoted in Tom Wyke, "What Caused 80 Whales to Beach Themselves on the Indian Coast?," *Daily Mail* (London), January 12, 2016, http://www.dailymail.co.uk/news /article-3395406/What-caused-80-whales-beach-Indian-coast-Mystery-dozens-animals-kill -returning-die-locals-dragged-sea.html.

93   Allison Lees Heater, e-mail interview with author, February 2016.

95   Charles Siebert, "Watching Whales Watching Us," *New York Times Magazine*, July 8, 2009, http://www.nytimes.com/2009/07/12/magazine/12whales-t.html?_r=0.

95–96 Sarah Wilson Finstuen, phone interview with author, April 2015.

96   Donna Hauser, phone interview with author, November 13, 2015.

96   Finstuen, interview.

97   Courtney Hann, phone interview with author, September 28, 2015.

98   Kristin Laidre, phone interview with author, November 19, 2015.

99   Leigh Torres, "Citizen Science: Benefits and Limitations for Marine Mammal Research and Education," group presentation at the 21st Biennial Conference on the Biology of Marine Mammals, San Francisco, December 17, 2015.

99   "New Tag Revolutionizes Whale Research, and Makes Them Partners in Science," *Science Daily*, December 23, 2016, http:// www.ScienceDaily.com/releases/2016/12 /161223115823.htm.

101   Joe Roman, quoted at *Voyaging in the Wake of the Whale* exhibit, Mystic Seaport, Connecticut, August 2015.

102   Ed Lyman, Hawaiian Islands Humpback Whale Marine Sanctuary page, NOAA, accessed August 25, 2016, http://hawaiihumpbackwhale.noaa.gov.

103   Ibid.

GLOSSARY

abundance: among whale scientists, this term refers to the number of whales in a given area of the ocean

baleen: plates of a fibrous protein called keratin that hang from the top of a whale's jaw. Whales use baleen to filter krill and other food out of the water and into their mouths.

biological classification: also called taxonomy, the process by which scientists group animals based on shared characteristics and classify them into a hierarchy (ranking), including levels such as kingdom, family, genus, and species

blowhole: a whale's nostril, positioned on the back of its head

blubber: a fatty layer that insulates a whale against cold and provides it with an energy source during long migrations

breach: the leap a whale makes out of the water. Scientists aren't sure why whales breach. Scientists suspect it may be a sign of joy, a method of communication, or a way to shake crusty barnacles off their bodies.

calf: a baby whale. Calving is when a mother whale gives birth.

cetacean: a member of the biological order of whales and dolphins

cetologist: a person who studies whales

commercial whaling: hunting whales for profit. Commercial whaling was very common among many nations in the nineteenth century and was outlawed in 1982 by the International Whaling Commission. Japan, Norway, and Iceland continue to whale commercially in defiance of the ban.

distribution: the location of whales and their range within a specific region

echolocation: an animal's use of sound to figure out an object's size and location. Whales make clicks and other noises, whose sound waves bounce off objects and travel back to the whale for interpretation.

grounds: the places where whales live or visit at certain times of the year for feeding, breeding, and birthing

hydrophone: a microphone that researchers use to pick up sound underwater

keystone animal: an animal at the top of the food chain whose health indicates the health of the whole food chain that supports it

marine sanctuary: an area of the ocean where animals such as whales are protected from hunting, pollution, and other dangers

megafauna: big animals. Animals that are considered megafauna may be the largest of their type, such as the biggest dragonflies or deer. Humans are megafauna. Big animals such as whales that are especially amazing are called charismatic megafauna.

model: also called a computer model, a research-based story whose plot changes according to data. For instance, scientists who know that gray whales have more babies in years when there is less ice can plug in data about ice cover and model or figure out how many calves will be born.

moratorium: a ban. The International Whaling Commission placed a ban on commercial whaling in 1982.

mysticete: baleen whales, a suborder of the order cetaceans. These whales have baleen plates in their mouths for sifting food.

necropsy: an examination a veterinarian or other scientist does on an animal after death to determine how or why an animal died and to assess its health prior to death

odontocete: toothed whales, a suborder of the order cetaceans. These whales have teeth for eating.

pod: a group of whales. Whales live and travel in pods of various numbers.

population: a subgroup of a species, for example, a group that lives in a certain region

situational awareness: scientific understanding of all the factors contributing to a whale's quality of life, including diet, weight, water quality, noise level, and other factors

species: a group of related animals based on similar genes. Species classification is the main unit of biological classification. Animals of the same species can mate with each other and have offspring.

Species in the Spotlight: a National Oceanic and Atmospheric Administration (NOAA) list of animals that are especially unique or potentially at risk of becoming endangered or extinct

stocks: populations of whales, or the number of whales that live in a particular habitat

subsistence hunting: hunting for food, not for profit. Most subsistence hunters in the United States and Canada are indigenous peoples with a long, historic hunting tradition.

SELECTED
BIBLIOGRAPHY

Garland, Ellen C., Anne W. Goldizen, Melinda L. Rekdahl, Rochelle Constantine, Claire Garrigue, Nan Daeschler Hauser, M. Michael Poole, Jooke Robbins, and Michael J. Noad. "Dynamic Horizontal Cultural Transmission of Humpback Whale Song at the Ocean Basin Scale." *Current Biology* 21, no. 8 (2011): 687–691. http://www.cell.com/current-biology/abstract/S0960-9822(11)00291-0?_returnURL=http%3A%2F%2Flinkinghub.elsevier.com%2Fretrieve%2Fpii%2FS0960982211002910%3Fshowall%3Dtrue.

Higham James, Lars Bejder, and Rob Williams. *Whale-Watching: Sustainable Tourism and Ecological Management*. Cambridge: Cambridge University Press, 2014.

Hoare, Philip. *The Whale: In Search of Giants of the Sea*. New York: Ecco, 2010.

Kraus, Scott D., and Rosalind M. Rolland, eds. *The Urban Whale*. Cambridge, MA: Harvard University Press, 2010.

Parsons, E. C. M. "The Negative Impacts of Whale-Watching," *Journal of Marine Biology* 2012 (2012). http://www.hindawi.com/journals/jmb/2012/807294/.

Sanders, Jon G., Annabel C. Beichman, Joe Roman, Jarrod J. Scott, David Emerson, James J. McCarthy, and Peter R. Girguis. "Baleen Whales Host a Unique Gut Microbiome with Similarities to Both Carnivores and Herbivores." *Nature Communications* 6 (September 22, 2015) doi:10.1038/ncomms9285.

Smith, Tim D., Randall R. Reeves, Elizabeth A. Josephson, and Judith N. Lund. "Spatial and Seasonal Distribution of American Whaling and Whales in the Age of Sail." *PLoS One* 7, no. 4 (April 27, 2012). http://www.ncbi.nlm.nih.gov/pmc/articles/PMC3338773/.

FURTHER INFORMATION

Books

Brakes, Philippa, and Mark Peter Simmons. *Whales and Dolphins: Cognition, Culture, Conservation and Human Perception*. New York: Earthscan, 2011. These essays by cetacean scientists discuss research and human understanding of whales and dolphins.

Chase, Owen. *The Wreck of the Whaleship Essex: A Narrative Account by Owen Chase, First Mate*. Edited by Iola Haverstick and Betty Shepard. Reprint, 1965. San Diego: Harcourt Brace, 1993. This is the true story of a whale that wrecks a whaling ship.

Cox, Lynne. *Grayson*. New York: Knopf, 2011. This inspiring book is the true story of a long-distance swimmer and the young whale that befriended her off the California coast.

George, Jean Craighead. *Ice Whale*. New York: Dial, 2014. This novel is about a bowhead whale and is set in and around a coastal Alaskan town.

Halls, Kelly Milner. *Dive into Danger*. Animal Rescue series. Minneapolis: Darby Creek, 2016. Milner's novel is about a fourteen-year-old boy, a whale, and the Marine Mammal Center in Sausalito, California.

L'Engle, Madeleine. *A Ring of Endless Light*. New York: Farrar, Straus & Giroux, 1980. This novel is about a girl working and swimming with dolphins in a lab environment and in the wild.

Markle, Sandra. *Animal Heroes: True Rescue Stories*. Minneapolis: Millbrook Press, 2009. Readers learn how dolphins and other animals use their senses and special abilities for the good of others.

McKissack, Patricia C. *Black Hands, White Sails*. Illustrated by Frederick McKissack. New York: Scholastic, 1999. This illustrated nonfiction book is still a great resource about diversity among whaling crews.

McPherson, Stephanie Sammartino. *Arctic Thaw: Climate Change and the Global Race for Energy Resources*. Minneapolis: Twenty-First Century Books, 2015. McPherson investigates the effect of climate change on the Arctic. Read about the race to secure new mineral resources and the way this is impacting fragile ecosystems and indigenous ways of life at the top of the world.

National Audubon Society. *National Audubon Society Guide to Marine Mammals of the World*. Illustrated by Pieter Folkens. New York: Alfred A. Knopf, 2002. Learn about cetaceans and how to identify them.

Roman, Joe. *Whale*. London: Reaktion Books, 2006. Roman discusses human-whale interactions from ancient times to the present.

Sommer, Bill, and Natalie Haney Tilghman. *A 52-Hertz Whale*. Minneapolis: Carolrhoda Lab, 2015. This YA novel tells the story of two young men, one of whom is obsessed with whales. The novel is told through the characters' exchange of e-mails.

Whiting, Emma Mayhew, and Henry Beetle Hough. *Whaling Wives*. Boston: Houghton Mifflin, 1953. This collection of biographies, diary entries, and letters from the wives of whalers includes many from women who went to sea with their husbands.

Cards and Games

The Phylo(mon) Project
>   http://phylogame.org
>   These printable trading cards and games involve whales and other species. The site was created as a real-world counterpart to Pokémon.

Southern Resident Community Orca Trading Cards
>   http://www.seattleaquarium.org/orcas
>   Each individual from J-, K-, and L- pods has a card showing distinguishing features and giving information about its life. The cards are available at the Seattle Aquarium online store.

Videos

Behind the Cove. Keiko Yagi, Tokyo: Yagi Film, 1:50. 2016.
>   This documentary explores commercial whaling in Japan, examining the issue from an animal rights' perspective. Yagi explores our choices about which animals are acceptable as a source of food for humans and which are not.

Demonstration of Ocean Alliance SnotBot Drone. Public Radio International (PRI), 1:32. August 12, 2015. http://www.pri.org/stories/2015-08-12/dont-let-name-fool-you-snotbot-drone -could-innovate-how-we-track-whales.
>   This PRI video describes SnotBot development.

Morphed: When Whales Had Legs. YouTube video, 45:00 minutes. Posted by "Ziff Edu," May 11, 2014. https://www.youtube.com/watch?v=-0CMx2VuP1U.
>   This video features scientists Hans Thewissen, Fred Spoor, and Philip Gingerich, eminent researchers on the natural history of whales.

New Video of a Nearly Unknown Whale Species. New England Aquarium, 0:25. October 26, 2015. http://news.neaq.org/2015/10/new-video-of-nearly-unknown-whale.html.
>   The newest species of whale, the Omura's whale, is featured.

"UAV Reveals Killer Whales in Striking Detail." NOAA, 12:31. Posted by Rich Press, October 21, 2015. http://www.nmfs.noaa.gov/podcasts/2015/10/uav_killer_whale.html.
>   Scientists are shown using drones to conduct whale research.

Whale's Eye View. National Geographic, 2:52. Accessed November 5, 2016.
>   http://video.nationalgeographic.com/video/crittercam/whale_humpback_crittercam.
>   Crittercam piggyback camera footage provides a unique perspective from the humped back of humpback whales.

Whales Weep Not. 5:48. Posted by James Donaldson, August 25, 2009. http:// iomarinemammals.wix.com/criomm#!about1/c1j38.
>   This documentary film includes the first underwater footage of sperm whales.

Audio

Bowhead Whale. Podcast by Ari Daniel Shapiro, Encyclopedia of Life, 5:13. March 20, 2013. http://eol.org/data_objects/24085255.
  This podcast includes an interview with Karen Romano Young discussing subsistence hunting in Alaska.

May, Michael. "Recordings That Made Waves: The Songs That Saved the Whales." *National Public Radio*, 5:39. December 26, 2014. http://www.npr.org/2014/12/26/373303726/recordings-that-made-waves-the-songs-that-saved-the-whales.
  This story about biologist Roger Payne includes links to recordings of whale songs.

Whalesong
  http://Whalesong.net
  Listen to live streaming of humpback whale songs off the coast of Maui.

Organizations

American Cetacean Society
  http://www.acsonline.org
  Headquartered in San Pedro, California, and founded in 1967, this is the world's first whale, dolphin, and porpoise conservation group. The society's mission is to protect cetacean habitats through public education, research grants, and conservation actions.

Ocean Alliance
  http://www.whale.org
  Roger Payne founded this research and conservation organization, which focuses on the world's oceans and marine creatures.

The Whale Trail
  http://www.thewhaletrail.org
  Find more than sixty sites along the West Coast of the United States and Canada—from California to British Columbia—for viewing orcas and other marine mammals from shore. This organization partners with others, such as the British Columbia Cetacean Sighting Network, the Washington Department of Fish and Wildlife, the National Marine Sanctuaries, and NOAA Fisheries to identify shore-viewing sites.

Websites

Antarctic Humpback Whale Catalogue
  https://www.flickr.com/photos/ahwc/collections/72157623423919294/
  The online catalogue is the result of an international effort to collect information about fifty-three hundred humpback whales in the Southern Ocean and lower latitudes. Scientists, naturalists, citizen scientists, and tourists contribute photographs.

Cetacean and Sound Mapping
> http://cetsound.noaa.gov
> Available on NOAA's website, the maps show where to look for sounds from natural and anthropogenic (human) sources. The data comes from an international collaboration among twenty-six marine experts in eleven countries.

Dinge & Goete (Things & Stuff)
> http://dingeengoete.blogspot.com/2013/07/this-day-in-history-jul-23-1982.html
> The July 23, 2013, blog entry by Juan Nel offers a great (and graphic) history of commercial whaling worldwide.

Marine Mammal Observer Association
> http://www.mmo-association.org
> This professional and commercial organization of Marine Mammal Observers (MMOs) and Passive Acoustic Monitoring (PAM) Operators is headquartered in London. Members work to protect marine mammals in industrial areas.

North Atlantic Humpback Whale Catalogue
> http://www.coa.edu/allied-whale/research/
> Learn about and search images of the eight thousand humpback whales that migrate between the Gulf of Maine and the Caribbean Sea.

Robots4Whales
> http://robots4whales.whoi.edu
> Mark Baumgartner's website enables viewers to follow gliders and figure out where they are and what they're studying.

Sea Sound Project, Salish Sea Hydrophone Network
> http://www.orcasound.net
> This project involves the work of scientists, educators, and citizens. At this website, listen to shipping noise, as it sounds to orcas in the Salish Sea (between Vancouver Island and Washington State).

Species in the Spotlight
> http://www.nmfs.noaa.gov/stories/2015/05/05_14_15species_in_the_spotlight.html
> NOAA and the National Marine Fisheries maintain this list of endangered animals at high risk of extinction. The list includes the Cook Inlet beluga whale and the Southern Resident killer whale.

Voices in the Sea
> http://cetus.ucsd.edu/voicesinthesea_org/index.html#
> This online multimedia exhibit comes from the Scripps Institution of Oceanography. Learn more about whales and their marine environment. Find out about whale conservation efforts and whale research.

Whale Hunt: The Narrative of a Voyage
> http://library.mysticseaport.org/initiative/PageImage.cfm?BibID=30775
> You can read diary excerpts from nineteenth-century teen whaler Nelson Cole Haley at this site.

INDEX

ABOUT THE AUTHOR

Karen Romano Young is a whale of a writer. She is the author of more than two dozen books for young readers, including *Across the Wide Ocean* and *Space Junk*, which garnered a starred review from *Kirkus Reviews*. She has written and illustrated articles, science comics, and books about whales and has traveled the oceans in search of them. She has never seen a wild orca or a blue whale, but once she saw a blue whale's spout and heard it breathe. This remains one of her most treasured moments.

PHOTO ACKNOWLEDGMENTS

The images in this book are used with the permission of: © iStockphoto.com/anttoniu, p. 2 (backgrounds throughout); © Kate Westaway/Stone Sub/Getty Images, p. 1; © Paul Souders/Corbis Documentary/Getty Images, p. 3; © blickwinkel/Alamy, pp. 4–5; © Flip Nicklin/Minden Pictures, p. 6; © iStockphoto.com/PacoRomero, p. 11; © Ron Sanford/Photo Researchers RM/Getty Images, p. 13; © Heritage Image Partnership Ltd/Alamy, p. 16; Courtesy of the New Bedford Whaling Museum, p. 18; © The Protected Art Archive/Alamy, p. 19; The Granger Collection, New York, p. 20; Courtesy of the New Bedford Whaling Museum, p. 22; © Nature Picture Library/Alamy, p. 23; © INTERFOTO/History, p. 28; © Leigh Calvez/Wikimedia Commons (license type), p. 31; © The Natural History Museum/Alamy, p. 33; © Steven J. Kazlowski/Alamy, p. 36; © robertharding/Alamy, p. 38; © Picture Adventure Expeditions/Barcroft Media/Getty Images, p. 42; © The Royal Society, p. 45; © Robert Lachman/Los Angeles Times/Getty Images, p. 46; © NICKLIN, FLIP/MINDEN PICTURES/National Geographic Stock, p. 49; © Chris & Monique Fallows/Minden Pictures, p. 50; © Laura Westlund/Independent Picture Service, pp. 54–55, 60, 82–83, 104–113; Flip Nicklin/Minden Pictures/Newscom, p. 56; © Todd Strand/Independent Picture Service, p. 58; © HenningPietsch/Wikimedia Commons (CC BY-SA 3.0), p. 63; © Arterra/UIG/Getty Images, p. 66; Image courtesy of The Ocean Exploration Trust via NOAA, p. 68; NOAA Fisheries, Vancouver Aquarium, p. 72; © Matthew Ryan Williams/The New York Times/Redux, p. 75; © George Skene/Orlando Sentinel/MCT/Getty Images, p. 76; © Moviestore collection Ltd/Alamy, p. 80; Photo courtesy of the U.S. Coast Guard via NOAA, p. 84; © REMKO DE WAAL/AFP/Getty Images, p. 90; Florida Fish and Wildlife Conservation Commission, taken under NOAA research permit #15488 via NOAA, p. 92; © Franco Banfi/WaterFrame/Getty Images, p. 94; © Paul Nicklen/National Geographic Creative/Getty Images, p. 98; © Image Source/Alamy, pp. 100–101; © John Hyde/First Light/Getty Images, p. 102.

Front cover: © Claude Huot/Alamy.